THE ALLURE OF GOODNESS AND LOVE

The Allure of Goodness and Love

Pope Francis in the United States

Complete Texts

LITURGICAL PRESS

Collegeville, Minnesota

www.litpress.org

Cover design by Monica Bokinskie. Cover photos: Catholic News Service.

All texts of Pope Francis © 2015 Libreria Editrice Vaticana. Used with permission.

1	2	3	4	5	6	7	8	9

Library of Congress Cataloging-in-Publication Data

Names: Francis, Pope, 1936– author.
Title: The allure of goodness and love : Pope Francis in the United States : complete texts.
Description: Collegeville, Minnesota : Liturgical Press, 2016.
Identifiers: LCCN 2015040133 | ISBN 9780814646670
Subjects: LCSH: Francis, Pope, 1936– —Travel—United States. | Papal visits—United States.
Classification: LCC BX1378.7 .A25 2016 | DDC 252/.02—dc23
LC record available at http://lccn.loc.gov/2015040133

Contents

Washington, DC
September 23–24, 2015

1 Welcoming Ceremony   3
South Lawn of the White House

2 Meeting with the Bishops of the United States of America   6
Cathedral of Saint Matthew

3 Holy Mass and Canonization of Blessed Fr. Junípero Serra   16
National Shrine of the Immaculate Conception

4 Visit to the Joint Session of the United States Congress   20
United States Capitol

5 Visit to the Charitable Center of St. Patrick Parish and
Meeting with the Homeless   30
St. Patrick in the City

New York City
September 24–25, 2015

6 Vespers with Priests and Religious   37
St. Patrick's Cathedral

7 Meeting with the Personnel of the United Nations   41
United Nations Headquarters

8 Meeting with the Members of the General Assembly
of the United Nations Organization   43
United Nations Headquarters

9 Interreligious Meeting   54
Ground Zero Memorial

10 Prayer of Remembrance of His Holiness Pope Francis   57
    Ground Zero Memorial

11 Meeting with Children and Immigrant Families   60
    Our Lady, Queen of Angels School

12 Holy Mass   63
    Madison Square Garden

Philadelphia
September 26–27, 2015

13 Holy Mass with Bishops, Clergy and Religious
    of Pennsylvania   69
    Cathedral of Sts. Peter and Paul

14 Meeting for Religious Liberty with the Hispanic Community
    and Other Immigrants   72
    Independence Mall

15 Prayer Vigil for the Festival of Families   77
    Benjamin Franklin Parkway

16 Meeting with Victims of Sexual Abuse   84
    St. Charles Borromeo Seminary

17 Meeting with Bishops Taking Part in the World Meeting
    of Families   86
    St. Charles Borromeo Seminary

18 Visit to Detainees   93
    Curran-Fromhold Correctional Facility

19 Closing Mass of the Eighth World Meeting of Families   96
    Benjamin Franklin Parkway

Postscript
September 27, 2015

20 In-Flight Press Conference   103
    Papal Flight

WASHINGTON, DC

SEPTEMBER 23–24, 2015

1

Welcoming Ceremony

Address of the Holy Father

South Lawn of the White House, Washington, DC
Wednesday, September 23, 2015

Good morning!
Mr. President,

I am deeply grateful for your welcome in the name of all Americans. As the son of an immigrant family, I am happy to be a guest in this country, which was largely built by such families. I look forward to these days of encounter and dialogue, in which I hope to listen to, and share, many of the hopes and dreams of the American people.

During my visit I will have the honor of addressing Congress, where I hope, as a brother of this country, to offer words of encouragement to those called to guide the nation's political future in fidelity to its founding principles. I will also travel to Philadelphia for the Eighth World Meeting of Families, to celebrate and support the institutions of marriage and the family at this, a critical moment in the history of our civilization.

Mr. President, together with their fellow citizens, American Catholics are committed to building a society which is truly tolerant and inclusive, to safeguarding the rights of individuals and communities, and to rejecting every form of unjust discrimination. With countless other people of goodwill, they are likewise concerned that efforts to build a just and wisely ordered society respect their deepest concerns and their right to religious liberty. That freedom remains one of America's most precious possessions. And, as my brothers, the United States Bishops, have reminded us, all are called to be vigilant, precisely as good citizens, to preserve and defend that freedom from everything that would threaten or compromise it.

Mr. President, I find it encouraging that you are proposing an initiative for reducing air pollution. Accepting the urgency, it seems clear to me also that climate change is a problem which can no longer be left to a future generation. When it comes to the care of our "common home," we are living at a critical moment of history. We still have time to make the changes needed to bring about "a sustainable and integral development, for we know that things can change" (*Laudato Sì* 13). Such change demands on our part a serious and responsible recognition not only of the kind of world we may be leaving to our children, but also to the millions of people living under a system which has overlooked them. Our common home has been part of this group of the excluded which cries out to heaven and which today powerfully strikes our homes, our cities and our societies. To use a telling phrase of the Reverend Martin Luther King, we can say that we have defaulted on a promissory note and now is the time to honor it.

We know by faith that "the Creator does not abandon us; he never forsakes his loving plan or repents of having created us. Humanity still has the ability to work together in building our common home" (*Laudato Sì* 13). As Christians inspired by this certainty, we wish to commit ourselves to the conscious and responsible care of our common home.

Mr. President, the efforts which were recently made to mend broken relationships and to open new doors to cooperation within our human family represent positive steps along the path of reconciliation, justice and freedom. I would like all men and women of goodwill in this great nation to support the efforts of the international community to protect the vulnerable in our world and to stimulate integral and inclusive models of development, so that our brothers and sisters everywhere may know the blessings of peace and prosperity which God wills for all his children.

Mr. President, once again I thank you for your welcome, and I look forward to these days in your country. God bless America!

2

Meeting with the Bishops
of the United States of America

Address of the Holy Father

Cathedral of Saint Matthew, Washington, DC
Wednesday, September 23, 2015

Dear Brother Bishops,

First of all, I wish to send a greeting to the Jewish community, our Jewish brothers and sisters, who today are celebrating Yom Kippur. May the Lord bless them with peace and help them to advance on the path of holiness, as we heard today in his word: "You shall be holy, for I am holy" (Lev 19:2).

I am pleased that we can meet at this point in the apostolic mission which has brought me to your country. I thank Cardinal Wuerl and Archbishop Kurtz for their kind words in your name. I am very appreciative of your welcome and the generous efforts made to help plan and organize my stay.

As I look out with affection at you, their pastors, I would like to embrace all the local Churches over which you exercise loving responsibility. I would ask you to share my affection and spiritual closeness with the People of God throughout this vast land.

The heart of the Pope expands to include everyone. To testify to the immensity of God's love is the heart of the mission entrusted to the Successor of Peter, the Vicar of the One who on the cross embraced the whole of mankind. May no member of Christ's Body and the American people feel excluded from the Pope's embrace. Wherever the name of Jesus is spoken, may the Pope's voice also be heard to affirm that: *"He is the Savior!"* From your great coastal cities to the plains of the Midwest, from the Deep South to the far reaches of the West, wherever your people gather in the Eucharistic assembly, may the Pope be not simply a name but a felt presence, sustaining the fervent plea of the Bride: *"Come, Lord!"*

Whenever a hand reaches out to do good or to show the love of Christ, to dry a tear or bring comfort to the lonely, to show the way to one who is lost or to console a broken heart, to help the fallen or to teach those thirsting for truth, to forgive or to offer a new start in God . . . know that the Pope is at your side, the Pope supports you. He puts his hand on your own, a hand wrinkled with age, but by God's grace still able to support and encourage.

My first word to you is one of thanksgiving to God for the power of the Gospel which has brought about remarkable growth of Christ's Church in these lands and enabled its generous contribution, past and present, to American society and to the world. I thank you most heartily for your generous solidarity with the Apostolic See and the support you give to the spread of the Gospel in many suffering areas of our world. I appreciate the unfailing commitment of the Church in America to the cause of life and that of the family, which is the primary reason for my present visit. I am well aware of the immense efforts you have made to welcome and integrate those immigrants who continue to look to America, like so many others before them, in the hope of enjoying its blessings of freedom and prosperity. I also appreciate the efforts which you are making to fulfill the Church's mission of education in schools at every level and in the charitable services offered by your numerous institutions. These works are often carried out without appreciation or support, often with heroic sacrifice, out of obedience to a divine mandate which we may not disobey.

I am also conscious of the courage with which you have faced difficult moments in the recent history of the Church in this country without fear of self-criticism and at the cost of mortification and great sacrifice. Nor have you been afraid to divest whatever is unessential in order to regain the authority and trust which is demanded of ministers of Christ and rightly expected by the faithful. I realize how much the pain of recent years has weighed upon you and I have supported your generous commitment to bring healing to victims—in the knowledge that in healing we too are healed—and to work to ensure that such crimes will never be repeated.

I speak to you as the Bishop of Rome, called by God in old age, and from a land which is also American, to watch over the unity of the universal Church and to encourage in charity the journey of all the particular Churches toward ever greater knowledge, faith and love of Christ. Reading over your names, looking at your faces, knowing the extent of your churchmanship and conscious of the devotion which you have always shown for the Successor of Peter, I must tell you that I do not feel a stranger in your midst. I am a native of a land which is also vast, with great open ranges, a land which, like your own, received the faith from itinerant missionaries. I too know how hard it is to sow the Gospel among people from different worlds, with hearts often hardened by the trials of a lengthy journey. Nor am I unaware of the efforts made over the years to build up the Church amid the prairies, mountains, cities and suburbs of a frequently inhospitable land, where frontiers are always provisional and easy answers do not always work. What does work is the combination of the epic struggle of the pioneers and the homely wisdom and endurance of the settlers. As one of your poets has put it, "strong and tireless wings" combined with the wisdom of one who "knows the mountains."[1]

I do not speak to you with my voice alone, but in continuity with the words of my predecessors. From the birth of this nation, when, following the American Revolution, the first diocese was erected in Baltimore, the Church of Rome has always been close to you; you have never lacked its constant assistance and encouragement. In recent decades, three Popes have visited you and left behind a remarkable legacy of teaching. Their words remain timely and have helped to inspire the long-term goals which you have set for the Church in this country.

It is not my intention to offer a plan or to devise a strategy. I have not come to judge you or to lecture you. I trust completely in the voice of the One who *"teaches all things"* (John 14:26). Allow me only, in the freedom of love, to speak to you as a brother among brothers. I have no wish to tell you what to do, because we all know what it is that the Lord asks of us. Instead, I would turn once again to the demanding task—ancient yet never new—of seeking out the paths we need to take and the spirit with which we need to work. Without claiming to be exhaustive, I would share with you some reflections which I consider helpful for our mission.

We are bishops of the Church, shepherds appointed by God to feed his flock. Our greatest joy is to be shepherds, and only shepherds, pastors with undivided hearts and selfless devotion. We need to preserve this joy and never let ourselves be robbed of it. The evil one roars like a lion, anxious to devour it, wearing us down in our resolve to be all that we are called to be, not for ourselves but in gift and service to the *"Shepherd of our souls"* (1 Pet 2:25).

The heart of our identity is to be sought in constant prayer, in preaching (Acts 6:4) and in shepherding the flock entrusted to our care (John 21:15-17; Acts 20:28-31).

Ours must not be just any kind of prayer, but familiar union with Christ, in which we daily encounter his gaze and sense that he is asking us the question: *"Who is my mother? Who are my brothers?"* (Mark 3:31-34). One in which we can calmly reply: *"Lord, here is your mother, here are your brothers! I hand them over to you; they are the ones whom you entrusted to me."* Such trusting union with Christ is what nourishes the life of a pastor.

It is not about preaching complicated doctrines, but joyfully proclaiming Christ who died and rose for our sake. The "style" of our mission should make our hearers feel that the message we preach is meant *"for us."* May the word of God grant meaning and fullness to every aspect of their lives; may the sacraments nourish them with that food which they cannot procure for themselves;

may the closeness of the shepherd make them long once again for the Father's embrace. Be vigilant that the flock may always encounter in the heart of their pastor that "taste of eternity" which they seek in vain in the things of this world. May they always hear from you a word of appreciation for their efforts to confirm in liberty and justice the prosperity in which this land abounds. At the same time, may you never lack the serene courage to proclaim that *"we must work not for the food which perishes, but for the food which endures for eternal life"* (John 6:27).

Shepherds who do not pasture themselves but are able to step back, away from the center, to "decrease," in order to feed God's family with Christ. Who keep constant watch, standing on the heights to look out with God's eyes on the flock which is his alone. Who ascend to the height of the cross of God's Son, the sole standpoint which opens to the shepherd the heart of his flock.

Shepherds who do not lower our gaze, concerned only with our concerns, but raise it constantly toward the horizons which God opens before us and which surpass all that we ourselves can foresee or plan. Who also watch over ourselves, so as to flee the temptation of narcissism, which blinds the eyes of the shepherd, makes his voice unrecognizable and his actions fruitless. In the countless paths which lie open to your pastoral concern, remember to keep focused on the core which unifies everything: *"You did it unto me"* (Matt 25:31-45).

Certainly it is helpful for a bishop to have the farsightedness of a leader and the shrewdness of an administrator, but we fall into hopeless decline whenever we confuse the power of strength with the strength of that powerlessness with which God has redeemed us. Bishops need to be lucidly aware of the battle between light and darkness being fought in this world. Woe to us, however, if we make of the cross a banner of worldly struggles and fail to realize that the price of lasting victory is allowing ourselves to be wounded and consumed (Phil 2:1-11).

We all know the anguish felt by the first Eleven, huddled together, assailed and overwhelmed by the fear of sheep scattered because the shepherd had been struck. But we also know that we have been given a spirit of courage and not of timidity. So we cannot let ourselves be paralyzed by fear.

I know that you face many challenges, and that the field in which you sow is unyielding and that there is always the temptation to give in to fear, to lick one's wounds, to think back on bygone times and to devise harsh responses to fierce opposition.

And yet we are promoters of the culture of encounter. We are living sacraments of the embrace between God's riches and our poverty. We are witnesses of the abasement and the condescension of God who anticipates in love our every response.

Dialogue is our method, not as a shrewd strategy but out of fidelity to the One who never wearies of visiting the marketplace, even at the eleventh hour, to propose his offer of love (Matt 20:1-16).

The path ahead, then, is dialogue among yourselves, dialogue in your presbyterates, dialogue with lay persons, dialogue with families, dialogue with society. I cannot ever tire of encouraging you to dialogue fearlessly. The richer the heritage which you are called to share with *parrhesia*, the more eloquent should be the humility with which you should offer it. Do not be afraid to set out on that "exodus" which is necessary for all authentic dialogue. Otherwise, we fail to understand the thinking of others, or to realize deep down that the brother or sister we wish to reach and redeem, with the power and the closeness of love, counts more than their positions, distant as they may be from what we hold as true and certain. Harsh and divisive language does not befit the tongue of a pastor, it has no place in his heart; although it may momentarily seem to win the day, only the enduring allure of goodness and love remains truly convincing.

We need to let the Lord's words echo constantly in our hearts: *"Take my yoke upon you, and learn from me, who am meek and humble of heart, and you will find refreshment for your souls"* (Matt 11:28-30). Jesus' yoke is a yoke of love and thus a pledge of refreshment. At times in our work we can be burdened by a sense of loneliness, and so feel the heaviness of the yoke that we forget that we have received it from the Lord. It seems to be ours alone, and so we drag it like weary oxen working a dry field, troubled by the thought that we are laboring in vain. We can forget the profound refreshment which is indissolubly linked to the One who has made us the promise.

We need to learn from Jesus, or better to learn Jesus, meek and humble; to enter into his meekness and his humility by contemplating his way of acting; to lead our Churches and our people—not infrequently burdened by the stress of everyday life—to the ease of the Lord's yoke. And to remember that Jesus' Church is kept whole not by *"consuming fire from heaven"* (Luke 9:54), but by the secret warmth of the Spirit, who *"heals what is wounded, bends what is rigid, straightens what is crooked."*

The great mission which the Lord gives us is one which we carry out in communion, collegially. The world is already so torn and divided, brokenness is now everywhere. Consequently, the Church, *"the seamless garment of the Lord"* cannot allow herself to be rent, broken or fought over.

Our mission as bishops is first and foremost to solidify unity, a unity whose content is defined by the Word of God and the one Bread of Heaven. With these two realities each of the Churches entrusted to us remains Catholic, because open to, and in communion with, all the particular Churches and with the Church of Rome which *"presides in charity."* It is imperative, therefore, to watch over that unity, to safeguard it, to promote it and to bear witness to it as a sign and instrument which, beyond every barrier, unites nations, races, classes and generations.

May the forthcoming Holy Year of Mercy, by drawing us into the fathomless depths of God's heart in which no division dwells, be for all of you a privileged moment for strengthening communion, perfecting unity, reconciling differences, forgiving one another and healing every rift, that your light may shine forth like *"a city built on a hill"* (Matt 5:14).

This service to unity is particularly important for this nation, whose vast material and spiritual, cultural and political, historical and human, scientific and technological resources impose significant moral responsibilities in a world which is seeking, confusedly and laboriously, new balances of peace, prosperity and integration. It is an essential part of your mission to offer to the United States of America the humble yet powerful leaven of communion. May all mankind know that the presence in its midst of the *"sacrament of unity"* (*Lumen Gentium* 1) is a guarantee that its fate is not decay and dispersion.

This kind of witness is a beacon whose light can reassure men and women sailing through the dark clouds of life that a sure haven awaits them, that they will not crash on the reefs or be overwhelmed by the waves. I encourage you, then, my brothers, to confront the challenging issues of our time. Ever present within each of them is life as gift and responsibility. The future freedom and dignity of our societies depends on how we face these challenges.

The innocent victim of abortion, children who die of hunger or from bombings, immigrants who drown in the search for a better tomorrow, the elderly or the sick who are considered a burden, the victims of terrorism, wars, violence and drug trafficking, the environment devastated by man's predatory relationship with nature—at stake in all of this is the gift of God, of which we are noble stewards but not masters. It is wrong, then, to look the other way or to remain silent. No less important is the Gospel of the Family, which in the World Meeting of Families in Philadelphia I will emphatically proclaim together with you and the entire Church.

These essential aspects of the Church's mission belong to the core of what we have received from the Lord. It is our duty to preserve and communicate them, even when the tenor of the times becomes resistant and even hostile to that message (*Evangelii Gaudium* 34–39). I urge you to offer this witness, with the means and creativity born of love, and with the humility of truth. It needs to be preached and proclaimed to those without, but also to find room in people's hearts and in the conscience of society.

To this end, it is important that the Church in the United States also be a humble home, a family fire which attracts men and women through the attractive light and warmth of love. As pastors, we know well how much darkness and cold there is in this world; we know the loneliness and the neglect experienced by many people, even amid great resources of communication and material wealth. We also know their fear in the face of life, their despair and the many forms of escapism to which it gives rise.

Consequently, only a Church which can gather around the family fire remains able to attract others. And not any fire, but the one which blazed forth on Easter morn. The risen Lord continues to challenge the Church's pastors through the quiet plea of so many of our brothers and sisters: *"Have you something to eat?"* We need to recognize the Lord's voice, as the apostles did on the shore of the lake of Tiberius (John 21:4-12). It becomes even more urgent to grow in the certainty that the embers of his presence, kindled in the fire of his passion, precede us and will never die out. Whenever this certainty weakens, we end up being caretakers of ash, and not guardians and dispensers of the true light and the warmth which causes our hearts to burn within us (Luke 24:32).

Before concluding, allow me to offer two recommendations which are close to my heart. The first refers to your fatherhood as bishops. Be pastors close to people, pastors who are neighbors and servants. Let this closeness be expressed in a special way towards your priests. Support them, so that they can continue to serve Christ with an undivided heart, for this alone can bring fulfillment to ministers of Christ. I urge you, then, not to let them be content with half-measures. Find ways to encourage their spiritual growth, lest they yield to the temptation to become notaries and bureaucrats, but instead reflect the motherhood of the Church, which gives birth to and raises her sons and daughters. Be vigilant lest they tire of getting up to answer those who knock on their door by night, just when they feel entitled to rest (Luke 11:5-8). Train them to be ready to stop, care for, soothe, lift up and assist those who, *"by chance,"* find themselves stripped of all they thought they had (Luke 10:29-37).

My second recommendation has to do with immigrants. I ask you to excuse me if in some way I am pleading my own case.

The Church in the United States knows like few others the hopes present in the hearts of these "pilgrims." From the beginning you have learned their languages, promoted their cause, made their contributions your own, defended their rights, helped them to prosper, and kept alive the flame of their faith. Even today, no American institution does more for immigrants than your Christian communities. Now you are facing this stream of Latin immigration which affects many of your dioceses. Not only as the Bishop of Rome, but also as a pastor from the South, I feel the need to thank and encourage you. Perhaps it will not be easy for you to look into their soul; perhaps you will be challenged by their diversity. But know that they also possess resources meant to be shared. So do not be afraid to welcome them. Offer them the warmth of the love of Christ and you will unlock the mystery of their heart. I am certain that, as so often in the past, these people will enrich America and its Church.

May God bless you and Our Lady watch over you! Thank you!

1. "In youth my wings were strong and tireless, / But I did not know the mountains. / In age I knew the mountains / But my weary wings could not follow my vision— / Genius is wisdom and youth." (Edgar Lee Masters, "Alexander Throckmorton," *Spoon River Anthology* [New York: Macmillan, 1921], 127).

3

Holy Mass and Canonization of Blessed Fr. Junípero Serra

Homily of His Holiness Pope Francis

National Shrine of the Immaculate Conception,
Washington, DC
Wednesday, September 23, 2015

Rejoice in the Lord always! I say it again, rejoice! These are striking words, words which impact our lives. Paul tells us to rejoice; he practically orders us to rejoice. This command resonates with the desire we all have for a fulfilling life, a meaningful life, a joyful life. It is as if Paul could hear what each one of us is thinking in his or her heart and to voice what we are feeling, what we are experiencing. Something deep within us invites us to rejoice and tells us not to settle for placebos which always keep us comfortable.

At the same time, though, we all know the struggles of everyday life. So much seems to stand in the way of this invitation to rejoice. Our daily routine can often lead us to a kind of glum apathy which gradually becomes a habit, with a fatal consequence: our hearts grow numb.

We don't want apathy to guide our lives . . . or do we? We don't want the force of habit to rule our life . . . or do we? So we ought to ask ourselves: What can we do to keep our heart from growing numb, becoming anesthetized? How do we make the joy of the Gospel increase and take deeper root in our lives?

Jesus gives the answer. He said to his disciples then and he says it to us now: Go forth! Proclaim! The joy of the Gospel is something to be experienced, something to be known and lived only through giving it away, through giving ourselves away.

The spirit of the world tells us to be like everyone else, to settle for what comes easy. Faced with this human way of thinking, "we must regain the conviction that we need one another, that we have a shared responsibility for others and for the world" (*Laudato Sì* 229). It is the responsibility to proclaim the message of Jesus. For the source of our joy is "an endless desire to show mercy, the fruit of our own experience of the power of the Father's infinite mercy" (*Evangelii Gaudium* 24). Go out to all, proclaim by anointing and anoint by proclaiming. This is what the Lord tells us today. He tells us:

A Christian finds joy in mission: Go out to people of every nation!

A Christian experiences joy in following a command: Go forth and proclaim the good news!

A Christian finds ever new joy in answering a call: Go forth and anoint!

Jesus sends his disciples out to all nations. To every people. We too were part of all those people of two thousand years ago. Jesus did not provide a short list of who is, or is not, worthy of receiving his message and his presence. Instead, he always embraced life as he saw it. In faces of pain, hunger, sickness and sin. In faces of wounds, of thirst, of weariness, doubt and pity. Far from expecting a pretty life, smartly-dressed and neatly groomed, he embraced life as he found it. It made no difference whether it was dirty, unkempt, broken. Jesus said: Go out and tell the good news to everyone. Go out and in my name embrace life as it is, and not as you think it should be. Go out to the highways and byways, go out to tell the good news fearlessly, without prejudice, without superiority, without condescension, to all those who have lost the joy of living. Go out to proclaim the merciful embrace of the Father. Go out to those who are burdened by pain and failure, who feel that their lives are empty, and proclaim the folly of a loving Father who wants to anoint them with the oil of hope, the oil of salvation. Go out to proclaim the good news that error, deceitful illusions and falsehoods do not have the last word in a person's life. Go out with the ointment which soothes wounds and heals hearts.

Mission is never the fruit of a perfectly planned program or a well-organized manual. Mission is always the fruit of a life which knows what it is to be found and healed, encountered and forgiven. Mission is born of a constant experience of God's merciful anointing.

The Church, the holy People of God, treads the dust-laden paths of history, so often traversed by conflict, injustice and violence, in order to encounter her children, our brothers and sisters. The holy and faithful People of God are not afraid of losing their way; they are afraid of becoming self-enclosed, frozen into élites, clinging to their own security. They know that self-enclosure, in all the many forms it takes, is the cause of so much apathy.

So let us go out, let us go forth to offer everyone the life of Jesus Christ (*Evangelii Gaudium* 49). The People of God can embrace everyone because we are the disciples of the One who knelt before his own to wash their feet (ibid., 24).

We are here today, we can be here today, because many people wanted to respond to that call. They believed that "life grows by being given away, and it weakens in isolation and comfort" (Aparecida Document 360). We are heirs to the bold missionary spirit of so many men and women who preferred not to be "shut up within structures which give us a false sense of security . . . within habits which make us feel safe, while at our door people are starving" (*Evangelii Gaudium* 49). We are indebted to a tradition, a chain of witnesses who have made it possible for the good news of the Gospel to be, in every generation, both "good" and "news."

Today we remember one of those witnesses who testified to the joy of the Gospel in these lands, Father Junípero Serra. He was the embodiment of "a Church which goes forth," a Church which sets out to bring everywhere the reconciling tenderness of God. Junípero Serra left his native land and its way of life. He was excited about blazing trails, going forth to meet many people, learning and valuing their particular customs and ways of life. He learned how to bring to birth and nurture God's life in the faces of everyone he met; he made them his brothers and sisters. Junípero sought to defend the dignity of the native community, to protect it from those who had mistreated and abused it. Mistreatment and wrongs which today still trouble us, especially because of the hurt which they cause in the lives of many people.

Father Serra had a motto which inspired his life and work, not just a saying, but above all a reality which shaped the way he lived: *siempre adelante!* Keep moving forward! For him, this was the way to continue experiencing the joy of the Gospel, to keep his heart from growing numb, from being anesthetized. He kept moving forward, because the Lord was waiting. He kept going, because his brothers and sisters were waiting. He kept going forward to the end of his life. Today, like him, may we be able to say: Forward! Let's keep moving forward!

4

Visit to the Joint Session of the United States Congress

Address of the Holy Father

United States Capitol, Washington, DC
Thursday, September 24, 2015

Mr. Vice-President,
Mr. Speaker,
Honorable Members of Congress,
Dear Friends,

I am most grateful for your invitation to address this Joint Session of Congress in "the land of the free and the home of the brave." I would like to think that the reason for this is that I too am a son of this great continent, from which we have all received so much and toward which we share a common responsibility.

Each son or daughter of a given country has a mission, a personal and social responsibility. Your own responsibility as members of Congress is to enable this country, by your legislative activity, to grow as a nation. You are the face of its people, their representatives. You are called to defend and preserve the dignity of your fellow citizens in the tireless and demanding pursuit of the common good, for this is the chief aim of all politics. A political society endures when it seeks, as a vocation, to satisfy common needs by stimulating the growth of all its members, especially those in situations of greater vulnerability or risk. Legislative activity is always based on care for the people. To this you have been invited, called and convened by those who elected you.

Yours is a work which makes me reflect in two ways on the figure of Moses. On the one hand, the patriarch and lawgiver of the people of Israel symbolizes the need of peoples to keep alive their sense of unity by means of just legislation. On the other, the figure of Moses leads us directly to God and thus to the transcendent dignity of the human being. Moses provides us with a good synthesis of your work: you are asked to protect, by means of the law, the image and likeness fashioned by God on every human face.

Today I would like not only to address you, but through you the entire people of the United States. Here, together with their representatives, I would like to take this opportunity to dialogue with the many thousands of men and women who strive each day to do an honest day's work, to bring home their daily bread, to save money and—one step at a time—to build a better life for their families. These are men and women who are not concerned simply with paying their taxes, but in their own quiet way sustain the life of society. They generate solidarity by their actions, and they create organizations which offer a helping hand to those most in need.

I would also like to enter into dialogue with the many elderly persons who are a storehouse of wisdom forged by experience, and who seek in many ways, especially through volunteer work, to share their stories and their insights. I know that many of them are retired, but still active; they keep working to build up this land. I also want to dialogue with all those young people who are working to realize their great and noble aspirations, who are not led astray by facile proposals, and who face difficult situations, often as a result of immaturity on the part of many adults. I wish to dialogue with all of you, and I would like to do so through the historical memory of your people.

My visit takes place at a time when men and women of goodwill are marking the anniversaries of several great Americans.

The complexities of history and the reality of human weakness notwithstanding, these men and women, for all their many differences and limitations, were able by hard work and self-sacrifice—some at the cost of their lives—to build a better future. They shaped fundamental values which will endure forever in the spirit of the American people. A people with this spirit can live through many crises, tensions and conflicts, while always finding the resources to move forward, and to do so with dignity. These men and women offer us a way of seeing and interpreting reality. In honoring their memory, we are inspired, even amid conflicts, and in the here and now of each day, to draw upon our deepest cultural reserves.

I would like to mention four of these Americans: Abraham Lincoln, Martin Luther King, Dorothy Day and Thomas Merton.

This year marks the one hundred and fiftieth anniversary of the assassination of President Abraham Lincoln, the guardian of liberty, who labored tirelessly that "this nation, under God, [might] have a new birth of freedom." Building a future of freedom requires love of the common good and cooperation in a spirit of subsidiarity and solidarity.

All of us are quite aware of, and deeply worried by, the disturbing social and political situation of the world today. Our world is increasingly a place of violent conflict, hatred and brutal atrocities, committed even in the name of God and of religion. We know that no religion is immune from forms of individual delusion or ideological extremism. This means that we must be especially attentive to every type of fundamentalism, whether religious or of any other kind. A delicate balance is required to combat violence perpetrated in the name of a religion, an ideology or an economic system, while also safeguarding religious freedom, intellectual freedom and individual freedoms. But there is another temptation which we must especially guard against: the simplistic reductionism which sees only good or evil; or, if you will, the righteous and sinners. The contemporary world, with its open wounds which affect so many of our brothers and sisters, demands that we confront every form of polarization which would divide it into these two camps. We know that in the attempt to be freed of the enemy without, we can be tempted to feed the enemy within. To imitate the hatred and violence of tyrants and murderers is the best way to take their place. That is something which you, as a people, reject.

Our response must instead be one of hope and healing, of peace and justice. We are asked to summon the courage and the intelligence to resolve today's many geopolitical and economic crises. Even in the developed world, the effects of unjust structures and actions are all too apparent. Our efforts must aim at restoring hope, righting wrongs, maintaining commitments, and thus promoting the well-being of individuals and of peoples. We must move forward together, as one, in a renewed spirit of fraternity and solidarity, cooperating generously for the common good.

The challenges facing us today call for a renewal of that spirit of cooperation, which has accomplished so much good throughout the history of the United States. The complexity, the gravity and the urgency of these challenges demand that we pool our resources and talents, and resolve to support one another, with respect for our differences and our convictions of conscience.

In this land, the various religious denominations have greatly contributed to building and strengthening society. It is important that today, as in the past, the voice of faith continue to be heard, for it is a voice of fraternity and love, which tries to bring out the best in each person and in each society. Such cooperation is a powerful resource in the battle to eliminate new global forms of slavery, born of grave injustices which can be overcome only through new policies and new forms of social consensus.

Here I think of the political history of the United States, where democracy is deeply rooted in the mind of the American people. All political activity must serve and promote the good of the human person and be based on respect for his or her dignity. "We hold these truths to be self-evident, that all men are created equal, that they are endowed by their Creator with certain unalienable rights, that among these are life, liberty and the pursuit of happiness" (Declaration of Independence, July 4, 1776). If politics must truly be at the service of the human person, it follows that it cannot be a slave to the economy and finance. Politics is, instead, an expression of our compelling need to live as one, in order to build as one the greatest common good: that of a community which sacrifices particular interests in order to share, in justice and peace, its goods, its interests, its social life. I do not underestimate the difficulty that this involves, but I encourage you in this effort.

Here too I think of the march which Martin Luther King led from Selma to Montgomery fifty years ago as part of the campaign to fulfill his "dream" of full civil and political rights for African Americans. That dream continues to inspire us all. I am happy that America continues to be, for many, a land of "dreams." Dreams which lead to action, to participation, to commitment. Dreams which awaken what is deepest and truest in the life of a people.

In recent centuries, millions of people came to this land to pursue their dream of building a future in freedom. We, the people of this continent, are not fearful of foreigners, because most of us were once foreigners. I say this to you as the son of immigrants, knowing that so many of you are also descended from immigrants. Tragically, the rights of those who were here long before us were not always respected. For those peoples and their nations, from the heart of American democracy, I wish to reaffirm my highest esteem and appreciation. Those first contacts were often turbulent and violent, but it is difficult to judge the past by the criteria of the present. Nonetheless, when the stranger in our midst appeals to us, we must not repeat the sins and the errors of the past. We must resolve now to live as nobly and as justly as possible, as we educate new generations not to turn their back on our "neighbors" and everything around us. Building a nation calls us to recognize that we must constantly relate to others, rejecting a mindset of hostility in order to adopt one of reciprocal subsidiarity, in a constant effort to do our best. I am confident that we can do this.

Our world is facing a refugee crisis of a magnitude not seen since the Second World War. This presents us with great challenges and many hard decisions. On this continent, too, thousands of persons are led to travel north in search of a better life for themselves and for their loved ones, in search of greater opportunities. Is this not what we want for our own children? We must not be taken aback by their numbers, but rather view them as persons, seeing their faces and listening to their stories, trying to respond as best we can to their situation. To respond in a way which is always humane, just and fraternal. We need to avoid a common temptation nowadays: to discard whatever proves troublesome. Let us remember the Golden Rule: "Do unto others as you would have them do unto you" (Matt 7:12).

This Rule points us in a clear direction. Let us treat others with the same passion and compassion with which we want to be treated. Let us seek for others the same possibilities which we seek for ourselves. Let us help others to grow, as we would like to be helped ourselves. In a word, if we want security, let us give security; if we want life, let us give life; if we want opportunities, let us provide opportunities. The yardstick we use for others will be the yardstick which time will use for us. The Golden Rule also reminds us of our responsibility to protect and defend human life at every stage of its development.

This conviction has led me, from the beginning of my ministry, to advocate at different levels for the global abolition of the death penalty. I am convinced that this way is the best, since every life is sacred, every human person is endowed with an inalienable dignity, and society can only benefit from the rehabilitation of those convicted of crimes. Recently my brother bishops here in the United States renewed their call for the abolition of the death penalty. Not only do I support them, but I also offer encouragement to all those who are convinced that a just and necessary punishment must never exclude the dimension of hope and the goal of rehabilitation.

In these times when social concerns are so important, I cannot fail to mention the Servant of God Dorothy Day, who founded the *Catholic Worker Movement*. Her social activism, her passion for justice and for the cause of the oppressed, were inspired by the Gospel, her faith, and the example of the saints.

How much progress has been made in this area in so many parts of the world! How much has been done in these first years of the third millennium to raise people out of extreme poverty! I know that you share my conviction that much more still needs to be done, and that in times of crisis and economic hardship a spirit of global solidarity must not be lost. At the same time I would encourage you to keep in mind all those people around us who are trapped in a cycle of poverty. They too need to be given hope. The fight against poverty and hunger must be fought constantly and on many fronts, especially in its causes. I know that many Americans today, as in the past, are working to deal with this problem.

It goes without saying that part of this great effort is the creation and distribution of wealth. The right use of natural resources, the proper application of technology and the harnessing of the spirit of enterprise are essential elements of an economy which seeks to be modern, inclusive and sustainable. "Business is a noble vocation, directed to producing wealth and improving the world. It can be a fruitful source of prosperity for the area in which it operates, especially if it sees the creation of jobs as an essential part of its service to the common good" (*Laudato Sì* 129). This common good also includes the earth, a central theme of the encyclical which I recently wrote in order to "enter into dialogue with all people about our common home" (ibid., 3). "We need a conversation which includes everyone, since the environmental challenge we are undergoing, and its human roots, concern and affect us all" (ibid., 14).

In *Laudato Sì*, I call for a courageous and responsible effort to "redirect our steps" (ibid., 61), and to avert the most serious effects of the environmental deterioration caused by human activity. I am convinced that we can make a difference and I have no doubt that the United States—and this Congress—have an important role to play. Now is the time for courageous actions and strategies, aimed at implementing a "culture of care" (ibid., 231) and "an integrated approach to combating poverty, restoring dignity to the excluded, and at the same time protecting nature" (ibid., 139). "We have the freedom needed to limit and direct technology" (ibid., 112); "to devise intelligent ways of . . . developing and limiting our power" (ibid., 78); and to put technology "at the service of another type of progress, one which is healthier, more human, more social, more integral" (ibid., 112). In this regard, I am confident that America's outstanding academic and research institutions can make a vital contribution in the years ahead.

A century ago, at the beginning of the Great War, which Pope Benedict XV termed a "pointless slaughter," another notable American was born: the Cistercian monk Thomas Merton. He remains a source of spiritual inspiration and a guide for many people. In his autobiography he wrote: "I came into the world. Free by nature, in the image of God, I was nevertheless the prisoner of my own violence and my own selfishness, in the image of the world into which I was born. That world was the picture of Hell, full of men like myself, loving God, and yet hating him; born to love him, living instead in fear of hopeless self-contradictory hungers." Merton was above all a man of prayer, a thinker who challenged the certitudes of his time and opened new horizons for souls and for the Church. He was also a man of dialogue, a promoter of peace between peoples and religions.

From this perspective of dialogue, I would like to recognize the efforts made in recent months to help overcome historic differences linked to painful episodes of the past. It is my duty to build bridges and to help all men and women, in any way possible, to do the same. When countries which have been at odds resume the path of dialogue—a dialogue which may have been interrupted for the most legitimate of reasons—new opportunities open up for all. This has required, and requires, courage and daring, which is not the same as irresponsibility. A good political leader is one who, with the interests of all in mind, seizes the moment in a spirit of openness and pragmatism. A good political leader always opts to initiate processes rather than possessing spaces (cf. *Evangelii Gaudium* 222–23).

Being at the service of dialogue and peace also means being truly determined to minimize and, in the long term, to end the many armed conflicts throughout our world. Here we have to ask ourselves: Why are deadly weapons being sold to those who plan to inflict untold suffering on individuals and society? Sadly, the answer, as we all know, is simply for money: money that is drenched in blood, often innocent blood. In the face of this shameful and culpable silence, it is our duty to confront the problem and to stop the arms trade.

Three sons and a daughter of this land, four individuals and four dreams: Lincoln, liberty; Martin Luther King, liberty in plurality and nonexclusion; Dorothy Day, social justice and the rights of persons; and Thomas Merton, the capacity for dialogue and openness to God.

Four representatives of the American people.

I will end my visit to your country in Philadelphia, where I will take part in the World Meeting of Families. It is my wish that throughout my visit the family should be a recurrent theme. How essential the family has been to the building of this country! And how worthy it remains of our support and encouragement! Yet I cannot hide my concern for the family, which is threatened, perhaps as never before, from within and without. Fundamental relationships are being called into question, as is the very basis of marriage and the family. I can only reiterate the importance and, above all, the richness and the beauty of family life.

In particular, I would like to call attention to those family members who are the most vulnerable, the young. For many of them, a future filled with countless possibilities beckons, yet so many others seem disoriented and aimless, trapped in a hopeless maze of violence, abuse and despair. Their problems are our problems. We cannot avoid them. We need to face them together, to talk about them and to seek effective solutions rather than getting bogged down in discussions. At the risk of oversimplifying, we might say that we live in a culture which pressures young people not to start a family, because they lack possibilities for the future. Yet this same culture presents others with so many options that they too are dissuaded from starting a family.

A nation can be considered great when it defends liberty as Lincoln did, when it fosters a culture which enables people to "dream" of full rights for all their brothers and sisters, as Martin Luther King sought to do; when it strives for justice and the cause of the oppressed, as Dorothy Day did by her tireless work, the fruit of a faith which becomes dialogue and sows peace in the contemplative style of Thomas Merton.

In these remarks I have sought to present some of the richness of your cultural heritage, of the spirit of the American people. It is my desire that this spirit continue to develop and grow, so that as many young people as possible can inherit and dwell in a land which has inspired so many people to dream.

God bless America!

Greeting of the Holy Father
from the Porch of the United States Capitol:
Good day to all of you. I thank you for your welcome and your presence. I thank the most important people here today: the children. I want to ask God to bless them. Lord, Father of us all, bless his people, bless each of them, bless their families, grant them what they need most. I ask you to pray for me and, if there are some among you who do not believe or cannot pray, I ask you please to wish me well. Thank you. Thank you very much. And God bless America!

5

Visit to the Charitable Center of St. Patrick Parish and Meeting with the Homeless

Greeting of the Holy Father

St. Patrick in the City, Washington, DC
Thursday, September 24, 2015

It is a pleasure to meet you. Good day. You are about to listen to two sermons, one in Spanish and the other in English. The first word I wish to say to you is "Thank you." Thank you for welcoming me and for your efforts to make this meeting possible.

Here I think of a person whom I love very much, someone who is, and has been, very important throughout my life. He has been a support and an inspiration. He is the one I go to whenever I am "in a fix." You make me think of Saint Joseph. Your faces remind me of his.

Joseph had to face some difficult situations in his life. One of them was the time when Mary was about to give birth, to have Jesus. The Bible tells us that, "while they were [in Bethlehem], the time came for her to deliver her child. And she gave birth to her firstborn son and wrapped him in bands of cloth, and laid him in a manger, because there was no place for them in the inn" (Luke 2:6-7).

The Bible is very clear about this: there was no room for them. I can imagine Joseph, with his wife about to have a child, with no shelter, no home, no place to stay. The Son of God came into this world as a homeless person. The Son of God knew what it was to start life without a roof over his head. We can imagine what Joseph must have been thinking. How is it that the Son of God has no home? Why are we homeless, why don't we have housing? These are questions which many of you may ask, and do ask, every day. Like Saint Joseph, you may ask: Why are we homeless, without a place to live? And those of us who do have a home, a roof over our heads, would also do well to ask: Why do these, our brothers and sisters, have no place to live? Why are these brothers and sisters of ours homeless?

Joseph's questions are timely even today; they accompany all those who throughout history have been, and are, homeless.

Joseph was someone who asked questions. But first and foremost, he was a man of faith. Faith gave Joseph the power to find light just at the moment when everything seemed dark. Faith sustained him amid the troubles of life. Thanks to faith, Joseph was able to press forward when everything seemed to be holding him back.

In the face of unjust and painful situations, faith brings us the light which scatters the darkness. As it did for Joseph, faith makes us open to the quiet presence of God at every moment of our lives, in every person and in every situation. God is present in every one of you, in each one of us.

I want to be very clear. There is no social or moral justification, no justification whatsoever, for lack of housing. There are many unjust situations, but we know that God is suffering with us, experiencing them at our side. He does not abandon us.

Jesus not only wanted to show solidarity with every person. He not only wanted everyone to experience his companionship, his help, his love. He identified with all those who suffer, who weep, who suffer any kind of injustice. He says this clearly: "I was hungry and you gave me food, I was thirsty and you gave me something to drink; I was a stranger and you welcomed me" (Matt 25:35),

Faith makes us know that God is at our side, that God is in our midst and his presence spurs us to charity. Charity is born of the call of a God who continues to knock on our door, the door of all people, to invite us to love, to compassion, to service of one another.

Jesus keeps knocking on our doors, the doors of our lives. He doesn't do this by magic, with special effects, with flashing lights and fireworks. Jesus keeps knocking on our door in the faces of our brothers and sisters, in the faces of our neighbors, in the faces of those at our side.

Dear friends, one of the most effective ways we have to help is that of prayer. Prayer unites us; it makes us brothers and sisters. It opens our hearts and reminds us of a beautiful truth which we sometimes forget. In prayer, we all learn to say "Father," "Dad." And when we say "Father," "Dad," we learn to see one another as brothers and sisters. In prayer, there are no rich or poor, there are sons and daughters, sisters and brothers. In prayer, there is no first or second class, there is brotherhood.

In prayer our hearts find the strength not to be cold and insensitive in the face of situations of injustice. In prayer, God keeps calling us, opening our hearts to charity.

How good it is for us to pray together. How good it is to encounter one another in this place where we see one another as brothers and sisters, where we realize that we need one another. Today I want to pray with you, I want to join with you, because I need your support, your closeness. I would like to invite you to pray together, for one another, with one another. That way we can keep helping one another to experience with joy that Jesus is in our midst, and that Jesus helps us to find solutions to the injustices which he himself already experienced. Not having a home.

Are you ready to pray together? I will begin in Spanish and you follow in English.

Our Father, who art in heaven. . . .

Before leaving you, I would like to give you God's blessing:
   The Lord bless you and keep you;
   the Lord make his face to shine upon you and be gracious
      to you;
   the Lord lift up his countenance upon you, and give you
      peace. (Num 6:24-26)
And, please, don't forget to pray for me. Thank you.

NEW YORK CITY

SEPTEMBER 24–25, 2015

— 6 —

Vespers with Priests and Religious
Homily of His Holiness Pope Francis

St. Patrick's Cathedral, New York
Thursday, September 24, 2015

I have two thoughts today for my Muslim brothers and sisters. First, my good wishes as you celebrate today the day of sacrifice. I wish my greetings could have been warmer. Second, my closeness, on account of the tragedy which your people experienced today in Mecca. In this moment of prayer, I join, and all of us join, in praying to God, our almighty and merciful Father.

We have heard the Apostle say: "There is a cause for rejoicing here," although "you may for a time have to suffer the distress of many trials" (1 Pet 1:6). These words remind us of something essential. Our vocation is to be lived in joy.

This beautiful Cathedral of Saint Patrick, built up over many years through the sacrifices of many men and women, can serve as a symbol of the work of generations of American priests and religious, and lay faithful who helped build up the Church in the United States. In the field of education alone, how many priests and religious in this country played a central role, assisting parents in handing on to their children the food that nourishes them for life! Many did so at the cost of extraordinary sacrifice and with heroic charity. I think for example of Saint Elizabeth Ann Seton, who founded the first free Catholic school for girls in America, or Saint John Neumann, the founder of the first system of Catholic education in the United States.

This evening, my brothers and sisters, I have come to join you—priests and men and women of consecrated life—in praying that our vocations will continue to build up the great edifice of God's Kingdom in this country. I know that, as a presbyterate in the midst of God's people, you suffered greatly in the not distant past by having to bear the shame of some of your brothers who harmed and scandalized the Church in the most vulnerable of her members . . . In the words of the Book of Revelation, I say that you "have come forth from the great tribulation" (Rev 7:14). I accompany you at this moment of pain and difficulty, and I thank God for your faithful service to his people. In the hope of helping you to persevere on the path of fidelity to Jesus Christ, I would like to offer two brief reflections.

The first concerns *the spirit of gratitude*. The joy of men and women who love God attracts others to him; priests and religious are called to find and radiate lasting satisfaction in their vocation. Joy springs from a grateful heart. Truly, we have received much, so many graces, so many blessings, and we rejoice in this. It will do us good to think back on our lives with the grace of remembrance. Remembrance of when we were first called, remembrance of the road travelled, remembrance of graces received . . . and, above all, remembrance of our encounter with Jesus Christ so often along the way. Remembrance of the amazement which our encounter with Jesus Christ awakens in our hearts. My brothers and sisters, men and women of consecrated life, and priests! Let us seek the grace of remembrance so as to grow in the spirit of gratitude. Let us ask ourselves: are we good at counting our blessings, or have we forgotten them?

A second area is *the spirit of hard work*. A grateful heart is spontaneously impelled to serve the Lord and to find expression in a life of commitment to our work. Once we come to realize how much God has given us, a life of self-sacrifice, of working for him and for others, becomes a privileged way of responding to his great love.

Yet, if we are honest, we know how easily this spirit of generous self-sacrifice can be dampened. There are a couple of ways that this can happen; both ways are examples of that "spiritual worldliness" which weakens our commitment as men and women of consecrated life to serve, and diminishes the wonder, the amazement, of our first encounter with Christ.

We can get caught up measuring the value of our apostolic works by the standards of efficiency, good management and outward success which govern the business world. Not that these things are unimportant! We have been entrusted with a great responsibility, and God's people rightly expect accountability from us. But the true worth of our apostolate is measured by the value it has in God's eyes. To see and evaluate things from God's perspective calls for constant conversion in the first days and years of our vocation and, need I say, it calls for great humility. The cross shows us a different way of measuring success. Ours is to plant the seeds: God sees to the fruits of our labors. And if at times our efforts and works seem to fail and produce no fruit, we need to remember that we are followers of Jesus . . . and his life, humanly speaking, ended in failure, in the failure of the cross.

The other danger comes when we become jealous of our free time, when we think that surrounding ourselves with worldly comforts will help us serve better. The problem with this reasoning is that it can blunt the power of God's daily call to conversion, to encounter with him. Slowly but surely, it diminishes our spirit of sacrifice, our spirit of renunciation and hard work. It also alienates people who suffer material poverty and are forced to make greater sacrifices than ourselves, without being consecrated. Rest is needed, as are moments of leisure and self-enrichment, but we need to learn how to rest in a way that deepens our desire to serve with generosity. Closeness to the poor, the refugee, the immigrant, the sick, the exploited, the elderly living alone, prisoners and all God's other poor, will teach us a different way of resting, one which is more Christian and generous.

Gratitude and hard work: these are two pillars of the spiritual life which I have wanted, this evening, to share with you priests and religious. I thank you for prayers and work, and the daily sacrifices you make in the various areas of your apostolate. Many of these are known only to God, but they bear rich fruit for the life of the Church.

In a special way I would like to express my esteem and my gratitude to the religious women of the United States. What would the Church be without you? Women of strength, fighters, with that spirit of courage which puts you in the front lines in the proclamation of the Gospel. To you, religious women, sisters and mothers of this people, I wish to say "thank you," a big thank you . . . and to tell you that I love you very much.

I know that many of you are in the front lines in meeting the challenges of adapting to an evolving pastoral landscape. Whatever difficulties and trials you face, I ask you, like Saint Peter, to be at peace and to respond to them as Christ did: he thanked the Father, took up his cross and looked forward!

Dear brothers and sisters, shortly, in a few minutes, we will sing the Magnificat. Let us commend to Our Lady the work we have been entrusted to do; let us join her in thanking God for the great things he has done, and for the great things he will continue to do in us and in those whom we have the privilege to serve. Amen.

— 7 —

Meeting with the Personnel of the United Nations

Greeting of the Holy Father

United Nations Headquarters, New York
Friday, September 25, 2015

Dear Friends,

On the occasion of my visit to the United Nations, I am pleased to greet you, the men and women who are, in many ways, the backbone of this Organization. I thank you for your welcome, and I am grateful for all that you have done to prepare for my visit. I would ask you also to offer my greetings to the members of your families and to your colleagues who could not be with us today.

The vast majority of the work done here is not of the kind that makes the news. Behind the scenes, your daily efforts make possible many of the diplomatic, cultural, economic and political initiatives of the United Nations, which are so important for meeting the hopes and expectations of the peoples who make up our human family. You are experts and experienced fieldworkers, officials and secretaries, translators and interpreters, cleaners and cooks, maintenance and security personnel. Thank you for all that you do!

Your quiet and devoted work not only contributes to the betterment of the United Nations. It also has great significance for you personally. For how we work expresses our dignity and the kind of persons we are.

Many of you have come to this city from countries the world over. As such, you are a microcosm of the peoples which this Organization represents and seeks to serve. Like so many other people worldwide, you are concerned about your children's welfare and education. You worry about the future of the planet, and what kind of a world we will leave for future generations. But today, and every day, I would ask each of you, whatever your capacity, to care for one another. Be close to one another, respect one another, and so embody among yourselves this Organization's ideal of a united human family, living in harmony, working not only *for* peace, but *in* peace; working not only *for* justice, but in a *spirit* of justice.

Dear friends, I bless each one of you from my heart. I will pray for you and your families, and I ask each of you, please, to remember to pray for me. And if any of you are not believers, I ask you to wish me well. God bless you all.

Thank you.

8

Meeting with the Members of the General Assembly of the United Nations Organization

Address of the Holy Father

United Nations Headquarters, New York
Friday, September 25, 2015

Mr. President,
Ladies and Gentlemen,

Good day. Once again, following a tradition by which I feel honored, the Secretary General of the United Nations has invited the Pope to address this distinguished assembly of nations. In my own name, and that of the entire Catholic community, I wish to express to you, Mr. Ban Ki-moon, my heartfelt gratitude. I greet the Heads of State and Heads of Government present, as well as the ambassadors, diplomats and political and technical officials accompanying them, the personnel of the United Nations engaged in this 70th Session of the General Assembly, the personnel of the various programs and agencies of the United Nations family, and all those who, in one way or another, take part in this meeting. Through you, I also greet the citizens of all the nations represented in this hall. I thank you, each and all, for your efforts in the service of mankind.

This is the fifth time that a Pope has visited the United Nations. I follow in the footsteps of my predecessors Paul VI, in 1965, John Paul II, in 1979 and 1995, and my most recent predecessor, now Pope Emeritus Benedict XVI, in 2008. All of them expressed their great esteem for the Organization, which they considered the appropriate juridical and political response to this present moment of history, marked by our technical ability to overcome distances and frontiers and, apparently, to overcome all natural limits to the exercise of power. An essential response, inasmuch as technological power, in the hands of nationalistic or falsely universalist ideologies, is capable of perpetrating tremendous atrocities. I can only reiterate the appreciation expressed by my predecessors, in reaffirming the importance which the Catholic Church attaches to this Institution and the hope which she places in its activities.

The United Nations is presently celebrating its seventieth anniversary. The history of this organized community of states is one of important common achievements over a period of unusually fast-paced changes. Without claiming to be exhaustive, we can mention the codification and development of international law, the establishment of international norms regarding human rights, advances in humanitarian law, the resolution of numerous conflicts, operations of peacekeeping and reconciliation, and any number of other accomplishments in every area of international activity and endeavor. All these achievements are lights which help to dispel the darkness of the disorder caused by unrestrained ambitions and collective forms of selfishness. Certainly, many grave problems remain to be resolved, yet it is also clear that, without all this international activity, mankind would not have been able to survive the unchecked use of its own possibilities. Every one of these political, juridical and technical advances is a path towards attaining the ideal of human fraternity and a means for its greater realization.

I also pay homage to all those men and women whose loyalty and self-sacrifice have benefitted humanity as a whole in these past seventy years. In particular, I would recall today those who gave their lives for peace and reconciliation among peoples, from Dag Hammarskjöld to the many United Nations officials at every level who have been killed in the course of humanitarian missions, and missions of peace and reconciliation.

Beyond these achievements, the experience of the past seventy years has made it clear that reform and adaptation to the times is always necessary in the pursuit of the ultimate goal of granting all countries, without exception, a share in, and a genuine and equitable influence on, decision-making processes. The need for greater equity is especially true in the case of those bodies with effective executive capability, such as the Security Council, the Financial Agencies and the groups or mechanisms specifically created to deal with economic crises. This will help limit every kind of abuse or usury, especially where developing countries are concerned. The International Financial Agencies should care for the sustainable development of countries and should ensure that they are not subjected to oppressive lending systems which, far from promoting progress, subject people to mechanisms which generate greater poverty, exclusion and dependence.

The work of the United Nations, according to the principles set forth in the Preamble and the first Articles of its founding Charter, can be seen as the development and promotion of the rule of law, based on the realization that justice is an essential condition for achieving the ideal of universal fraternity. In this context, it is helpful to recall that the limitation of power is an idea implicit in the concept of law itself. To give to each his own, to cite the classic definition of justice, means that no human individual or group can consider itself absolute, permitted to bypass the dignity and the rights of other individuals or their social groupings. The effective distribution of power (political, economic, defense-related, technological, etc.) among a plurality of subjects, and the creation of a juridical system for regulating claims and interests, are one concrete way of limiting power. Yet today's world presents us with many false rights and—at the same time—broad sectors which are vulnerable, victims of power badly exercised: for example, the natural environment and the vast ranks of the excluded. These sectors are closely interconnected and made increasingly fragile by dominant political and economic relationships. That is why their rights must be forcefully affirmed, by working to protect the environment and by putting an end to exclusion.

First, it must be stated that a true "right of the environment" does exist, for two reasons. First, because we human beings are part of the environment. We live in communion with it, since the environment itself entails ethical limits which human activity must acknowledge and respect. Man, for all his remarkable gifts, which "are signs of a uniqueness which transcends the spheres of physics and biology" (*Laudato Sì* 81), is at the same time a part of these spheres. He possesses a body shaped by physical, chemical and biological elements, and can only survive and develop if the ecological environment is favorable. Any harm done to the environment, therefore, is harm done to humanity. Second, because every creature, particularly a living creature, has an intrinsic value, in its existence, its life, its beauty and its interdependence with other creatures. We Christians, together with the other monotheistic religions, believe that the universe is the fruit of a loving decision by the Creator, who permits man respectfully to use creation for the good of his fellow men and for the glory of the Creator; he is not authorized to abuse it, much less to destroy it. In all religions, the environment is a fundamental good (cf. ibid.).

The misuse and destruction of the environment are also accompanied by a relentless process of exclusion. In effect, a selfish and boundless thirst for power and material prosperity leads both to the misuse of available natural resources and to the exclusion of the weak and disadvantaged, either because they are differently abled (handicapped), or because they lack adequate information and technical expertise, or are incapable of decisive political action. Economic and social exclusion is a complete denial of human fraternity and a grave offense against human rights and the environment. The poorest are those who suffer most from such offenses, for three serious reasons: they are cast off by society, forced to live off what is discarded and suffer unjustly from the abuse of the environment. They are part of today's widespread and quietly growing "culture of waste."

The dramatic reality of this whole situation of exclusion and inequality, with its evident effects, has led me, in union with the entire Christian people and many others, to take stock of my grave responsibility in this regard and to speak out, together with all those who are seeking urgently-needed and effective solutions. The adoption of the *2030 Agenda for Sustainable Development* at the World Summit, which opens today, is an important sign of hope. I am similarly confident that the *Paris Conference on Climatic Change* will secure fundamental and effective agreements.

Solemn commitments, however, are not enough, although they are certainly a necessary step toward solutions. The classic definition of justice which I mentioned earlier contains as one of its essential elements a constant and perpetual will: *Iustitia est constans et perpetua voluntas ius sum cuique tribuendi*. Our world demands of all government leaders a will which is effective, practical and constant, concrete steps and immediate measures for preserving and improving the natural environment and thus putting an end as quickly as possible to the phenomenon of social and economic exclusion, with its baneful consequences: human trafficking, the marketing of human organs and tissues, the sexual exploitation of boys and girls, slave labor, including prostitution, the drug and weapons trade, terrorism and international organized crime. Such is the magnitude of these situations and their toll on innocent lives, that we must avoid every temptation to fall into a declarationist nominalism which would assuage our consciences. We need to ensure that our institutions are truly effective in the struggle against all these scourges.

The number and complexity of the problems require that we possess technical instruments of verification. But this involves two risks. We can rest content with the bureaucratic exercise of drawing up long lists of good proposals—goals, objectives and statistics—or we can think that a single theoretical and aprioristic solution will provide an answer to all the challenges. It must never be forgotten that political and economic activity is only effective when it is understood as a prudential activity, guided by a perennial concept of justice and constantly conscious of the fact that, above and beyond our plans and programmes, we are dealing with real men and women who live, struggle and suffer, and are often forced to live in great poverty, deprived of all rights.

To enable these real men and women to escape from extreme poverty, we must allow them to be dignified agents of their own destiny. Integral human development and the full exercise of human dignity cannot be imposed. They must be built up and allowed to unfold for each individual, for every family, in communion with others, and in a right relationship with all those areas in which human social life develops—friends, communities, towns and cities, schools, businesses and unions, provinces, nations, etc. This presupposes and requires the right to education— also for girls (excluded in certain places)—which is ensured first and foremost by respecting and reinforcing the primary right of the family to educate its children, as well as the right of churches and social groups to support and assist families in the education of their children. Education conceived in this way is the basis for the implementation of the *2030 Agenda* and for reclaiming the environment.

At the same time, government leaders must do everything possible to ensure that all can have the minimum spiritual and material means needed to live in dignity and to create and support a family, which is the primary cell of any social development. In practical terms, this absolute minimum has three names: lodging, labor, and land; and one spiritual name: spiritual freedom, which includes religious freedom, the right to education and all other civil rights.

For all this, the simplest and best measure and indicator of the implementation of the new *Agenda* for development will be effective, practical and immediate access, on the part of all, to essential material and spiritual goods: housing, dignified and properly remunerated employment, adequate food and drinking water; religious freedom and, more generally, spiritual freedom and education. These pillars of integral human development have a common foundation, which is the right to life and, more generally, what we could call the right to existence of human nature itself.

The ecological crisis, and the large-scale destruction of biodiversity, can threaten the very existence of the human species. The baneful consequences of an irresponsible mismanagement of the global economy, guided only by ambition for wealth and power, must serve as a summons to a forthright reflection on man: "man is not only a freedom which he creates for himself. Man does not create himself. He is spirit and will, but also nature" (Benedict XVI, *Address to the Bundestag,* September 22, 2011, cited in *Laudato Sì* 6). Creation is compromised "where we ourselves have the final word. . . . The misuse of creation begins when we no longer recognize any instance above ourselves, when we see nothing else but ourselves" (idem., *Address to the Clergy of the Diocese of Bolzano-Bressanone,* 6 August 2008, cited in ibid.). Consequently, the defense of the environment and the fight against exclusion demand that we recognize a moral law written into human nature itself, one which includes the natural difference between man and woman (cf. *Laudato Sì* 155), and absolute respect for life in all its stages and dimensions (cf. ibid., 123, 136).

Without the recognition of certain incontestable natural ethical limits and without the immediate implementation of those pillars of integral human development, the ideal of "saving succeeding generations from the scourge of war" (*Charter of the United Nations,* Preamble), and "promoting social progress and better standards of life in larger freedom" (ibid.), risks becoming an unattainable illusion, or, even worse, idle chatter which serves as a cover for all kinds of abuse and corruption, or for carrying out an ideological colonization by the imposition of anomalous models and lifestyles which are alien to people's identity and, in the end, irresponsible.

War is the negation of all rights and a dramatic assault on the environment. If we want true integral human development for all, we must work tirelessly to avoid war between nations and peoples.

To this end, there is a need to ensure the uncontested rule of law and tireless recourse to negotiation, mediation and arbitration, as proposed by the *Charter of the United Nations*, which constitutes truly a fundamental juridical norm. The experience of these seventy years since the founding of the United Nations in general, and in particular the experience of these first fifteen years of the third millennium, reveal both the effectiveness of the full application of international norms and the ineffectiveness of their lack of enforcement. When the *Charter of the United Nations* is respected and applied with transparency and sincerity, and without ulterior motives, as an obligatory reference point of justice and not as a means of masking spurious intentions, peaceful results will be obtained. When, on the other hand, the norm is considered simply as an instrument to be used whenever it proves favorable, and to be avoided when it is not, a true Pandora's Box is opened, releasing uncontrollable forces which gravely harm defenseless populations, the cultural milieu and even the biological environment.

The Preamble and the first Article of the *Charter of the United Nations* set forth the foundations of the international juridical framework: peace, the pacific solution of disputes and the development of friendly relations between the nations. Strongly opposed to such statements, and in practice denying them, is the constant tendency to the proliferation of arms, especially weapons of mass distraction, such as nuclear weapons. An ethics and a law based on the threat of mutual destruction—and possibly the destruction of all mankind—are self-contradictory and an affront to the entire framework of the United Nations, which would end up as "nations united by fear and distrust." There is urgent need to work for a world free of nuclear weapons, in full application of the nonproliferation Treaty, in letter and spirit, with the goal of a complete prohibition of these weapons.

The recent agreement reached on the nuclear question in a sensitive region of Asia and the Middle East is proof of the potential of political goodwill and of law, exercised with sincerity, patience and constancy. I express my hope that this agreement will be lasting and efficacious, and bring forth the desired fruits with the cooperation of all the parties involved.

In this sense, hard evidence is not lacking of the negative effects of military and political interventions which are not coordinated between members of the international community. For this reason, while regretting to have to do so, I must renew my repeated appeals regarding the painful situation of the entire Middle East, North Africa and other African countries, where Christians, together with other cultural or ethnic groups, and even members of the majority religion who have no desire to be caught up in hatred and folly, have been forced to witness the destruction of their places of worship, their cultural and religious heritage, their houses and property, and have faced the alternative either of fleeing or of paying for their adhesion to good and to peace by their own lives, or by enslavement.

These realities should serve as a grave summons to an examination of conscience on the part of those charged with the conduct of international affairs. Not only in cases of religious or cultural persecution, but in every situation of conflict, as in Ukraine, Syria, Iraq, Libya, South Sudan and the Great Lakes region, real human beings take precedence over partisan interests, however legitimate the latter may be. In wars and conflicts there are individual persons, our brothers and sisters, men and women, young and old, boys and girls who weep, suffer and die. Human beings who are easily discarded when our response is simply to draw up lists of problems, strategies and disagreements.

As I wrote in my letter to the Secretary General of the United Nations on August 9, 2014, "the most basic understanding of human dignity compels the international community, particularly through the norms and mechanisms of international law, to do all that it can to stop and to prevent further systematic violence against ethnic and religious minorities" and to protect innocent peoples.

Along the same lines I would mention another kind of conflict which is not always so open, yet is silently killing millions of people. Another kind of war experienced by many of our societies as a result of the narcotics trade. A war which is taken for granted and poorly fought. Drug trafficking is by its very nature accompanied by trafficking in persons, money laundering, the arms trade, child exploitation and other forms of corruption. A corruption which has penetrated to different levels of social, political, military, artistic and religious life, and, in many cases, has given rise to a parallel structure which threatens the credibility of our institutions.

I began this speech recalling the visits of my predecessors. I would hope that my words will be taken above all as a continuation of the final words of the address of Pope Paul VI; although spoken almost exactly fifty years ago, they remain ever timely. I quote: "The hour has come when a pause, a moment of recollection, reflection, even of prayer, is absolutely needed so that we may think back over our common origin, our history, our common destiny. The appeal to the moral conscience of man has never been as necessary as it is today. . . . For the danger comes neither from progress nor from science; if these are used well, they can help to solve a great number of the serious problems besetting mankind" (Address to the United Nations Organization, October 4, 1965). Among other things, human genius, well applied, will surely help to meet the grave challenges of ecological deterioration and of exclusion. As Paul VI said: "The real danger comes from man, who has at his disposal ever more powerful instruments that are as well fitted to bring about ruin as they are to achieve lofty conquests" (ibid.).

The common home of all men and women must continue to rise on the foundations of a right understanding of universal fraternity and respect for the sacredness of every human life, of every man and every woman, the poor, the elderly, children, the infirm, the unborn, the unemployed, the abandoned, those considered disposable because they are only considered as part of a statistic. This common home of all men and women must also be built on the understanding of a certain sacredness of created nature.

Such understanding and respect call for a higher degree of wisdom, one which accepts transcendence, self-transcendence, rejects the creation of an all-powerful élite, and recognizes that the full meaning of individual and collective life is found in self-less service to others and in the sage and respectful use of creation for the common good. To repeat the words of Paul VI, "the edifice of modern civilization has to be built on spiritual principles, for they are the only ones capable not only of supporting it, but of shedding light on it" (ibid.).

El Gaucho Martín Fierro, a classic of literature in my native land, says: "Brothers should stand by each other, because this is the first law; keep a true bond between you always, at every time—because if you fight among yourselves, you'll be devoured by those outside."

The contemporary world, so apparently connected, is experiencing a growing and steady social fragmentation, which places at risk "the foundations of social life" and consequently leads to "battles over conflicting interests" (*Laudato Sì* 229).

The present time invites us to give priority to actions which generate new processes in society, so as to bear fruit in significant and positive historical events (cf. *Evangelii Gaudium* 223). We cannot permit ourselves to postpone "certain agendas" for the future. The future demands of us critical and global decisions in the face of worldwide conflicts which increase the number of the excluded and those in need.

The praiseworthy international juridical framework of the United Nations Organization and of all its activities, like any other human endeavor, can be improved, yet it remains necessary; at the same time it can be the pledge of a secure and happy future for future generations. And so it will, if the representatives of the States can set aside partisan and ideological interests, and sincerely strive to serve the common good. I pray to Almighty God that this will be the case, and I assure you of my support and my prayers, and the support and prayers of all the faithful of the Catholic Church, that this Institution, all its member States, and each of its officials, will always render an effective service to mankind, a service respectful of diversity and capable of bringing out, for sake of the common good, the best in each people and in every individual. God bless you all. Thank you.

— 9 —

Interreligious Meeting
Address of the Holy Father

Ground Zero Memorial, New York
Friday, September 25, 2015

I feel many different emotions standing here at Ground Zero, where thousands of lives were taken in a senseless act of destruction. Here grief is palpable. The water we see flowing towards that empty pit reminds us of all those lives which fell prey to those who think that destruction, tearing down, is the only way to settle conflicts. It is the silent cry of those who were victims of a mindset which knows only violence, hatred and revenge. A mindset which can only cause pain, suffering, destruction and tears.

The flowing water is also a symbol of our tears. Tears at so much devastation and ruin, past and present. This is a place where we shed tears, we weep out of a sense of helplessness in the face of injustice, murder, and the failure to settle conflicts through dialogue. Here we mourn the wrongful and senseless loss of innocent lives because of the inability to find solutions which respect the common good. This flowing water reminds us of yesterday's tears, but also of all the tears still being shed today.

A few moments ago I met some of the families of the fallen first responders. Meeting them made me see once again how acts of destruction are never impersonal, abstract or merely material. They always have a face, a concrete story, names. In those family members, we see the face of pain, a pain which still touches us and cries out to heaven.

At the same time, those family members showed me the other face of this attack, the other face of their grief: the power of love and remembrance. A remembrance that does not leave us empty and withdrawn. The name of so many loved ones are written around the towers' footprints. We can see them, we can touch them, and we can never forget them.

Here, amid pain and grief, we also have a palpable sense of the heroic goodness which people are capable of, those hidden reserves of strength from which we can draw. In the depths of pain and suffering, you also witnessed the heights of generosity and service. Hands reached out, lives were given. In a metropolis which might seem impersonal, faceless, lonely, you demonstrated the powerful solidarity born of mutual support, love and self-sacrifice. No one thought about race, nationality, neighborhoods, religion or politics. It was all about solidarity, meeting immediate needs, brotherhood. It was about being brothers and sisters. New York City firemen walked into the crumbling towers, with no concern for their own well-being. Many succumbed; their sacrifice enabled great numbers to be saved.

This place of death became a place of life too, a place of saved lives, a hymn to the triumph of life over the prophets of destruction and death, to goodness over evil, to reconciliation and unity over hatred and division.

In this place of sorrow and remembrance I am filled with hope, as I have the opportunity to join with leaders representing the many religious traditions which enrich the life of this great city. I trust that our presence together will be a powerful sign of our shared desire to be a force for reconciliation, peace and justice in this community and throughout the world. For all our differences and disagreements, we can experience a world of peace. In opposing every attempt to create a rigid uniformity, we can and must build unity on the basis of our diversity of languages, cultures and religions, and lift our voices against everything which would stand in the way of such unity. Together we are called to say "no" to every attempt to impose uniformity and "yes" to a diversity accepted and reconciled.

This can only happen if we uproot from our hearts all feelings of hatred, vengeance and resentment. We know that that is only possible as a gift from heaven. Here, in this place of remembrance, I would ask everyone together, each in his or her own way, to spend a moment in silence and prayer. Let us implore from on high the gift of commitment to the cause of peace. Peace in our homes, our families, our schools and our communities. Peace in all those places where war never seems to end. Peace for those faces which have known nothing but pain. Peace throughout this world which God has given us as the home of all and a home for all. Simply PEACE. Let us pray in silence.

(a moment of silence)

In this way, the lives of our dear ones will not be lives which will one day be forgotten. Instead, they will be present whenever we strive to be prophets not of tearing down but of building up, prophets of reconciliation, prophets of peace.

Prayer of Remembrance
of His Holiness Pope Francis

Ground Zero Memorial, New York
Friday, September 25, 2015

O God of love, compassion, and healing,
look on us, people of many different faiths
and religious traditions,
who gather today on this hallowed ground,
the scene of unspeakable violence and pain.

We ask you in your goodness
to give eternal light and peace
to all who died here:
the heroic first-responders:
our fire fighters, police officers,
emergency service workers
and Port Authority personnel,
along with all the innocent men and women
who were victims of this tragedy
simply because their work or service
brought them here on September 11.

We ask you, in your compassion,
to bring healing to those who,
because of their presence here fourteen years ago,
continue to suffer from injuries and illness.

Heal, too, the pain of still-grieving families
and all who lost loved ones in this tragedy.
Give them strength to continue their lives
with courage and hope.

We are mindful as well
of those who suffered death, injury, and loss
on the same day at the Pentagon
and in Shanksville, Pennsylvania.
Our hearts are one with theirs
as our prayer embraces their pain and suffering.

God of peace, bring your peace to our violent world:
peace in the hearts of all men and women
and peace among the nations of the earth.
Turn to your way of love
those whose hearts and minds
are consumed with hatred,
and who justify killing in the name of religion.

God of understanding,
overwhelmed by the magnitude of this tragedy,
we seek your light and guidance
as we confront such terrible events.

Grant that those whose lives were spared
may live so that the lives lost here
may not have been lost in vain.

Comfort and console us, strengthen us in hope,
and give us the wisdom and courage
to work tirelessly for a world
where true peace and love reign
among nations and in the hearts of all.

— 11 —

Meeting with Children and Immigrant Families

Address of the Holy Father

Our Lady, Queen of Angels School, Harlem, New York
Friday, September 25, 2015

Dear Brothers and Sisters,
Good afternoon!

I am very happy to be with you today, together with this big family which surrounds you. I see your teachers, your parents and your family members. Thank you for letting me come, and I ask pardon from your teachers for "stealing" a few minutes of their class time. I know that you don't mind that!

They tell me that one of the nice things about this school, about your work, is that some students come from other places, and many from other countries. That is nice! Even though I know that it is not easy to have to move and find a new home, to meet new neighbors and new friends. It is not easy, but you have to start. At the beginning it can be pretty hard. Often you have to learn a new language, adjust to a new culture, even a new climate. There is so much to learn! And not just homework, but so other many things too.

The good thing is that we also make new friends. This is very important, the new friends we make. We meet people who open doors for us, who are kind to us. They offer us friendship and understanding, and they try to help us not to feel like strangers, foreigners. People work hard to help us feel at home. Even if we sometimes think back on where we came from, we meet good people who help us feel at home. How nice it is to feel that our school, or the places where we gather, are a second home. This is not only important for you, but also for your families. School then ends up being one big family. A family where, together with our mothers and fathers, our grandparents, our teachers and friends, we learn to help one another, to share our good qualities, to give the best of ourselves, to work as a team, for that is very important, and to pursue our dreams.

Very near here is a very important street named after a man who did a lot for other people. I want to talk a little bit about him. He was the Reverend Martin Luther King. One day he said, "I have a dream." His dream was that many children, many people could have equal opportunities. His dream was that many children like you could get an education. He dreamed that many men and women, like yourselves, could lift their heads high, in dignity and self-sufficiency. It is beautiful to have dreams and to be able to fight for our dreams. Don't ever forget this.

Today we want to keep dreaming. We celebrate all the opportunities which enable you, and us adults too, not to lose the hope of a better world with greater possibilities. So many of the people I have met are also dreaming with you, they are dreaming of this. That is why they are doing this work. They are involved in your lives to help you move ahead. All of us dream. Always. I know that one of the dreams of your parents and teachers, and all those who help them—and Cardinal Dolan too, who is a good fellow—is that you can grow up and be happy. Here I see you smiling. Keep smiling and help bring joy to everyone you meet. It isn't always easy. Every home has its problems, difficult situations, sickness, but never stop dreaming so you can be happy.

All of you here, children and adults, have a right to dream and I am very happy that here in school, in your friends and your teachers, in all who are here to help, you can find the support you need. Wherever there are dreams, wherever there is joy, Jesus is always present. Always. But who is it that sows sadness, that sows mistrust, envy, evil desires? What is his name? The devil. The devil always sows sadness, because he doesn't want us to be happy; he doesn't want us to dream. Wherever there is joy, Jesus is always present. Because Jesus is joy, and he wants to help us to feel that joy every day of our lives.

Before going, I would like to give you some homework. Can I? It is just a little request, but a very important one. Please don't forget to pray for me, so that I can share with many people the joy of Jesus. And let us also pray that many other people can share joy like your own, whenever you feel supported, helped and counseled, even when there are problems. Even then, we still feel peace in our hearts, because Jesus never abandons us.

May God bless every one of you today and may Our Lady watch over all of you. Thank you.

Impromptu remarks

Don't you know any songs? Don't you know how to sing? Let's see, who is the bravest one here . . . *(song)*. Thank you very much. Now, all together . . . one song, and then we can all pray the Our Father *(song, followed by the Our Father)*. May almighty God bless you, the Father, the Son, and the Holy Spirit. *(Amen)*. Pray for me! Don't forget the homework!

12

Holy Mass

Homily of His Holiness Pope Francis

Madison Square Garden, New York
Friday, September 25, 2015

We are in Madison Square Garden, a place synonymous with this city. This is the site of important athletic, artistic and musical events attracting people not only from this city, but from the whole world. In this place, which represents both the variety and the common interests of so many different people, we have listened to the words: "The people who walked in darkness have seen a great light" (Isa 9:1).

The people who walked—caught up in their activities and routines, amid their successes and failures, their worries and expectations—have seen a great light. The people who walked—with all their joys and hopes, their disappointments and regrets—have seen a great light.

In every age, the People of God are called to contemplate this light. A light for the nations, as the elderly Simeon joyfully expressed it. A light meant to shine on every corner of this city, on our fellow citizens, on every part of our lives.

"The people who walked in darkness have seen a great light." One special quality of God's people is their ability to see, to

contemplate, even in "moments of darkness," the light which
Christ brings. God's faithful people can see, discern and contemplate his living presence in the midst of life, in the midst of the
city. Together with the prophet Isaiah, we can say: The people
who walk, breathe and live in the midst of smog, have seen a
great light, have experienced a breath of fresh air.

Living in a big city is not always easy. A multicultural context
presents many complex challenges. Yet big cities are a reminder
of the hidden riches present in our world: in the diversity of its
cultures, traditions and historical experiences. In the variety of
its languages, costumes and cuisine. Big cities bring together all
the different ways which we human beings have discovered to
express the meaning of life, wherever we may be.

But big cities also conceal the faces of all those people who don't
appear to belong, or are second-class citizens. In big cities, beneath
the roar of traffic, beneath "the rapid pace of change," so many
faces pass by unnoticed because they have no "right" to be there,
no right to be part of the city. They are the foreigners, the children
who go without schooling, those deprived of medical insurance,
the homeless, the forgotten elderly. These people stand at the
edges of our great avenues, in our streets, in deafening anonymity. They become part of an urban landscape which is more and
more taken for granted, in our eyes, and especially in our hearts.

Knowing that Jesus still walks our streets, that he is part of the
lives of his people, that he is involved with us in one vast history
of salvation, fills us with hope. A hope which liberates us from the
forces pushing us to isolation and lack of concern for the lives of
others, for the life of our city. A hope which frees us from empty
"connections," from abstract analyses, or sensationalist routines.
A hope which is unafraid of involvement, which acts as a leaven
wherever we happen to live and work. A hope which makes us
see, even in the midst of smog, the presence of God as he continues to walk the streets of our city. Because God is in the city.

What is it like, this light travelling through our streets? How
do we encounter God, who lives with us amid the smog of our

cities? How do we encounter Jesus, alive and at work in the daily life of our multicultural cities?

The prophet Isaiah can guide us in this process of "learning to see." He speaks of the light which is Jesus. And now he presents Jesus to us as "Wonderful Counselor, the Mighty God, the Everlasting Father, the Prince of Peace." In this way, he introduces us to the life of the Son, so that his life can be our life.

Wonderful Counselor. The Gospels tell us how many people came up to Jesus to ask: "Master, what must we do?" The first thing that Jesus does in response is to propose, to encourage, to motivate. He keeps telling his disciples to go, to go out. He urges them to go out and meet others where they really are, not where we think they should be. Go out, again and again, go out without fear, go out without hesitation. Go out and proclaim this joy which is for all the people.

The Mighty God. In Jesus, God himself became Emmanuel, God-with-us, the God who walks alongside us, who gets involved in our lives, in our homes, in the midst of our "pots and pans," as Saint Teresa of Jesus liked to say.

The Everlasting Father. No one or anything can separate us from his Love. Go out and proclaim, go out and show that God is in your midst as a merciful Father who himself goes out, morning and evening, to see if his son has returned home and, as soon as he sees him coming, runs out to embrace him. This is beautiful. An embrace which wants to take up, purify and elevate the dignity of his children. A Father who, in his embrace, is "glad tidings to the poor, healing to the afflicted, liberty to captives, comfort to those who mourn" (Isa 61:1-2).

Prince of Peace. Go out to others and share the good news that God, our Father, walks at our side. He frees us from anonymity, from a life of emptiness, and brings us to the school of encounter. He removes us from the fray of competition and self-absorption, and he opens before us the path of peace. That peace which is born of accepting others, that peace which fills our hearts whenever we look upon those in need as our brothers and sisters.

God is living in our cities. The Church is living in our cities. God and the Church living in our cities want to be like yeast in the dough, to relate to everyone, to stand at everyone's side, proclaiming the marvels of the Wonderful Counselor, the Mighty God, the Eternal Father, the Prince of Peace.

"The people who walked in darkness have seen a great light." And we, as Christians, are witnesses to this.

PHILADELPHIA

SEPTEMBER 26–27, 2015

Holy Mass with Bishops, Clergy and Religious of Pennsylvania

Homily of His Holiness Pope Francis

Cathedral of Sts. Peter and Paul, Philadelphia
Saturday, September 26, 2015

This morning I learned something about the history of this beautiful Cathedral: the story behind its high walls and windows. I would like to think, though, that the history of the Church in this city and state is really a story not about building walls, but about breaking them down. It is a story about generation after generation of committed Catholics going out to the peripheries, and building communities of worship, education, charity and service to the larger society.

That story is seen in the many shrines which dot this city, and the many parish churches whose towers and steeples speak of God's presence in the midst of our communities. It is seen in the efforts of all those dedicated priests, religious and laity who for over two centuries have ministered to the spiritual needs of the poor, the immigrant, the sick and those in prison. And it is seen in the hundreds of schools where religious brothers and sisters trained children to read and write, to love God and neighbor, and to contribute as good citizens to the life of American society. All of this is a great legacy which you have received, and which you have been called to enrich and pass on.

Most of you know the story of Saint Katharine Drexel, one of the great saints raised up by this local Church. When she spoke to Pope Leo XIII of the needs of the missions, the Pope—he was a very wise Pope!—asked her pointedly: "What about you? What are you going to do?" Those words changed Katharine's life, because they reminded her that, in the end, every Christian man and woman, by virtue of baptism, has received a mission. Each one of us has to respond, as best we can, to the Lord's call to build up his Body, the Church.

"What about you?" I would like to dwell on two aspects of these words in the context of our specific mission to transmit the joy of the Gospel and to build up the Church, whether as priests, deacons, or men and women who belong to institutes of consecrated life.

First, those words—"What about you?"—were addressed to a young person, a young woman with high ideals, and they changed her life. They made her think of the immense work that had to be done, and to realize that she was being called to do her part. How many young people in our parishes and schools have the same high ideals, generosity of spirit, and love for Christ and the Church! I ask you: Do we challenge them? Do we make space for them and help them to do their part? To find ways of sharing their enthusiasm and gifts with our communities, above all in works of mercy and concern for others? Do we share our own joy and enthusiasm in serving the Lord?

One of the great challenges facing the Church in this generation is to foster in all the faithful a sense of personal responsibility for the Church's mission, and to enable them to fulfill that responsibility as missionary disciples, as a leaven of the Gospel in our world. This will require creativity in adapting to changed situations, carrying forward the legacy of the past not primarily by maintaining our structures and institutions, which have served us well, but above all by being open to the possibilities which the Spirit opens up to us and communicating the joy of the Gospel, daily and in every season of our life.

"What about you?" It is significant that these words of the elderly Pope were also addressed to a lay woman. We know that the future of the Church in a rapidly changing society will call, and even now calls, for a much more active engagement on the part of the laity. The Church in the United States has always devoted immense effort to the work of catechesis and education. Our challenge today is to build on those solid foundations and to foster a sense of collaboration and shared responsibility in planning for the future of our parishes and institutions. This does not mean relinquishing the spiritual authority with which we have been entrusted; rather, it means discerning and employing wisely the manifold gifts which the Spirit pours out upon the Church. In a particular way, it means valuing the immense contribution which women, lay and religious, have made and continue to make, in the life of our communities.

Dear brothers and sisters, I thank you for the way in which each of you has answered Jesus' question which inspired your own vocation: "What about you?" I encourage you to be renewed in the joy and wonder of that first encounter with Jesus, and to draw from that joy renewed fidelity and strength. I look forward to being with you in these days and I ask you to bring my affectionate greetings to those who could not be with us, especially the many elderly priests and men and women religious who join us in spirit.

During these days of the World Meeting of Families, I would ask you in a particular way to reflect on our ministry to families, to couples preparing for marriage, and to our young people. I know how much is being done in the local Churches to respond to the needs of families and to support them in their journey of faith. I ask you to pray fervently for them, and for the deliberations of the forthcoming Synod on the Family.

Now, with gratitude for all we have received, and with confident assurance in all our needs, we turn to Mary, our Blessed Mother. With a mother's love, may she intercede for the growth of the Church in America in prophetic witness to the power of her Son's Cross to bring joy, hope and strength into our world. I pray for each of you, and I ask you, please, to pray for me.

— ·— 14 —· —

Meeting for Religious Liberty with the Hispanic Community and Other Immigrants

Address of the Holy Father

Independence Mall, Philadelphia
Saturday, September 26, 2015

Dear Friends,

Good afternoon. One of the highlights of my visit is to stand here, before Independence Hall, the birthplace of the United States of America. It was here that the freedoms which define this country were first proclaimed. The Declaration of Independence stated that all men and women are created equal, that they are endowed by their Creator with certain inalienable rights, and that governments exist to protect and defend those rights. Those ringing words continue to inspire us today, even as they have inspired peoples throughout the world to fight for the freedom to live in accordance with their dignity.

History also shows that these or any truths must constantly be reaffirmed, reappropriated and defended. The history of this nation is also the tale of a constant effort, lasting to our own day, to embody those lofty principles in social and political life.

We remember the great struggles which led to the abolition of slavery, the extension of voting rights, the growth of the labor movement, and the gradual effort to eliminate every kind of racism and prejudice directed at further waves of new Americans. This shows that, when a country is determined to remain true to its principles, those founding principles based on respect for human dignity, it is strengthened and renewed. When a country is mindful of its roots, it keeps growing, it is renewed and it continues to embrace newcomers, new individuals and new peoples.

All of us benefit from remembering our past. A people which remembers does not repeat past errors; instead, it looks with confidence to the challenges of the present and the future. Remembrance saves a people's soul from whatever or whoever would attempt to dominate it or to use it for their own interests. When individuals and communities are guaranteed the effective exercise of their rights, they are not only free to realize their potential, they also, through their talents and their hard work, contribute to the welfare and enrichment of society as a whole.

In this place which is symbolic of the American way, I would like to reflect with you on the right to religious freedom. It is a fundamental right which shapes the way we interact socially and personally with our neighbors whose religious views differ from our own. The ideal of interreligious dialogue, where all men and women, from different religious traditions, can speak to one another without arguing. This is what religious freedom allows.

Religious freedom certainly means the right to worship God, individually and in community, as our consciences dictate. But religious liberty, by its nature, transcends places of worship and the private sphere of individuals and families. Because religion itself, the religious dimension, is not a subculture; it is part of the culture of every people and every nation.

Our various religious traditions serve society primarily by the message they proclaim. They call individuals and communities to worship God, the source of all life, liberty and happiness. They remind us of the transcendent dimension of human existence and our irreducible freedom in the face of any claim to absolute power. We need but look at history—we always benefit from looking at history—especially the history of the last century, to see the atrocities perpetrated by systems which claimed to build one or another "earthly paradise" by dominating peoples, subjecting them to apparently indisputable principles and denying them any kind of rights. Our rich religious traditions seek to offer meaning and direction, "they have an enduring power to open new horizons, to stimulate thought, to expand the mind and heart" (*Evangelii Gaudium* 256). They call to conversion, reconciliation, concern for the future of society, self-sacrifice in the service of the common good, and compassion for those in need. At the heart of their spiritual mission is the proclamation of the truth and dignity of the human person and all human rights.

Our religious traditions remind us that, as human beings, we are called to acknowledge an Other, who reveals our relational identity in the face of every effort to impose "a uniformity to which the egotism of the powerful, the conformism of the weak, or the ideology of the utopian would seek to impose on us" (M. de Certeau).

In a world where various forms of modern tyranny seek to suppress religious freedom, or, as I said earlier, to try to reduce it to a subculture without right to a voice in the public square, or to use religion as a pretext for hatred and brutality, it is imperative that the followers of the various religious traditions join their voices in calling for peace, tolerance and respect for the dignity and the rights of others.

We live in an age subject to the "globalization of the technocratic paradigm" (*Laudato Sì* 106), which consciously aims at a one-dimensional uniformity and seeks to eliminate all differences and traditions in a superficial quest for unity. The religions thus have the right and the duty to make clear that it is possible to build a society where "a healthy pluralism which respects differences and values them as such" (*Evangelii Gaudium* 255) is a "precious ally in the commitment to defending human dignity . . . and a path to peace in our world," wounded as it is by wars (ibid., 257).

The Quakers who founded Philadelphia were inspired by a profound evangelical sense of the dignity of each individual and the ideal of a community united by brotherly love. This conviction led them to found a colony which would be a haven of religious freedom and tolerance. That sense of fraternal concern for the dignity of all, especially the weak and the vulnerable, became an essential part of the American spirit. During his visit to the United States in 1987, Saint John Paul II paid moving homage to this, reminding all Americans that: "The ultimate test of your greatness is the way you treat every human being, but especially the weakest and most defenseless ones" (*Farewell Address*, September 19, 1987, 3).

I take this opportunity to thank all those, of whatever religion, who have sought to serve God, the God of peace, by building cities of brotherly love, by caring for our neighbors in need, by defending the dignity of God's gift, the gift of life in all its stages, and by defending the cause of the poor and the immigrant. All too often, those most in need of our help, everywhere, are unable to be heard. You are their voice, and many of you—men and women—have faithfully made their cry heard. In this witness, which frequently encounters powerful resistance, you remind American democracy of the ideals for which it was founded, and that society is weakened whenever and wherever injustice prevails.

Just now I spoke of the trend towards globalization. Globalization is not evil. On the contrary, the tendency to become globalized is good; it brings us together. What can be evil is how it happens. If a certain kind of globalization claims to make everyone uniform, to level everyone out, that globalization destroys the rich gifts and uniqueness of each person and each people. But a globalization which attempts to bring everyone together while respecting the uniqueness and gifts of each person or people is a good globalization; it helps all of us to grow, and it brings peace. I like to use a geometrical image for this. If globalization is a sphere, where every point is equidistant from the center, it cancels everything out; it is not good. But if globalization is like a polyhedron, where everything is united but each element keeps its own identity, then it is good; it causes a people to grow, it bestows dignity and it grants rights to all.

Among us today are members of America's large Hispanic population, as well as representatives of recent immigrants to the United States. Many of you have emigrated (I greet you warmly!) to this country at great personal cost, in the hope of building a new life. Do not be discouraged by whatever hardships you face. I ask you not to forget that, like those who came here before you, you bring many gifts to this nation. Please, you should never be ashamed of your traditions. Do not forget the lessons you learned from your elders, which are something you can bring to enrich the life of this American land. I repeat, do not be ashamed of what is part of you, your life blood. You are also called to be responsible citizens, and to contribute fruitfully—as those who came before you did with such fortitude—to the life of the communities in which you live. I think in particular of the vibrant faith which so many of you possess, the deep sense of family life and all those other values which you have inherited. By contributing your gifts, you will not only find your place here, you will help to renew society from within. Do not forget what took place here over two centuries ago. Do not forget that Declaration which proclaimed that all men and women are created equal, that they are endowed by their Creator with certain inalienable rights and that governments exist in order to protect and defend those rights.

Dear friends, I thank you for your warm welcome and for joining me here today. Let us preserve freedom. Let us cherish freedom. Freedom of conscience, religious freedom, the freedom of each person, each family, each people, which is what gives rise to rights. May this country and each of you be renewed in gratitude for the many blessings and freedoms that you enjoy. And may you defend these rights, especially your religious freedom, for it has been given to you by God himself. May he bless you all. I ask you, please, say a little prayer for me. Thank you.

— · — 15 — · —

Prayer Vigil for the Festival of Families

Address of the Holy Father

Benjamin Franklin Parkway, Philadelphia
Saturday, September 26, 2015

Dear Brothers and Sisters,
Dear Families,

I thank those who offered their witness and those who brought us joy through their art, through beauty, which is the way to God. Beauty brings us to God. And a truthful witness brings us to God, because God is also truth. He is beauty and he is truth. A witness intended to help others is good, it makes us good, because God is goodness. It brings us to God. All that is good, all that is true and all that is beautiful brings us to God. Because God is good, God is beauty, God is truth.

I thank all of you. Those who spoke to us and the presence of everyone here, which is itself a witness. A truthful witness that family life is something worthwhile, and that a society grows stronger and better, it grows in beauty and it grows in truth, when it rises on the foundation of the family.

A young person once asked me—you know how young people ask hard questions!—"Father, what did God do before he created the world?" Believe me, I had a hard time answering that one.

I told him what I am going to tell you now. Before he created the world, God loved, because God is love. The love he had within himself, the love between the Father and the Son, in the Holy Spirit, was so great, so overflowing—I'm not sure if this is theologically precise, but you will get what I am saying—that love was so great that God could not be selfish. He had to go out from himself, in order to have someone to love outside of himself. So God created the world. God made this wonderful world in which we live and which, since we are not too smart, we are now in the process of destroying.

But the most beautiful thing God made—so the Bible tells us—was the family. He created man and woman. And he gave them everything. He entrusted the world to them: "Grow, multiply, cultivate the earth, make it bear fruit, let it grow." All the love he put into that marvelous creation, he entrusted to a family.

Let's go back a bit. All the love God has in himself, all the beauty God has in himself, all the truth God has in himself, he entrusts to the family. A family is truly a family when it is capable of opening its arms to receive all that love. Of course the Garden of Eden is long gone; life has its problems; men and women—through the wiles of the devil—experienced division. And all that love which God gave us was practically lost. And in no time, the first crime was committed, the first fratricide. Brother kills brother: war. God's love, beauty and truth, and on the other hand the destructiveness of war: we are poised between those two realities even today. It is up to us to choose, to decide which way to go.

But let's go back. When the man and his wife went astray and walked away from God, God did not leave them alone. Such was his love. So great was his love that he began to walk with mankind, he began to walk alongside his people, until the right time came and then he gave the greatest demonstration of love: his Son. And where did he send his Son? To a palace, to a city, to an office building? He sent him to a family. God came into the world in a family. And he could do this because that family was a family with a heart open to love, a family whose doors were open.

We can think of Mary, a young woman. She couldn't believe it: "How can this be?" But once it was explained to her, she obeyed. We think of Joseph, full of dreams for making a home; then along comes this surprise which he doesn't understand. He accepts, he obeys. And in the loving obedience of this woman, Mary, and this man, Joseph, we have a family into which God comes. God always knocks on the doors of our hearts. He likes to do that. He goes out from within. But do you know what he likes best of all? To knock on the doors of families. And to see families which are united, families which love, families which bring up their children, educating them and helping them to grow, families which build a society of goodness, truth and beauty.

We are celebrating the festival of families. The family has a divine identity card. Do you see what I mean? God gave the family an identity card, so that families could be places in our world where his truth, love and beauty could continue to take root and grow. Some of you may say to me: "Father, you can say that because you're not married!" Certainly, in the family there are difficulties. In families we argue. In families sometimes we throw dishes. In families children cause headaches. I'm not going to say anything about mothers-in-law! Families always, always, have crosses. Always. Because the love of God, the Son of God, also asked us to follow him along this way. But in families also, the cross is followed by resurrection, because there too the Son of God leads us. So the family is—if you excuse the word—a workshop of hope, of the hope of life and resurrection, since God was the one who opened this path. Then too, there are children. Children are hard work. When we were children, we were hard work. Sometimes back home I see some of my staff who come to work with rings under their eyes. They have a one- or two-month-old baby. And I ask them: "Didn't you get any sleep?" And they say: "No, the baby cried all night." In families, there are difficulties, but those difficulties are resolved by love. Hatred doesn't resolve any difficulty. Divided hearts do not resolve difficulties. Only love is capable of resolving difficulty. Love is a celebration, love is joy, love is perseverance.

I don't want to keep on talking because it will go on too long, but I did want to stress two little points about the family. I would ask you to think about them. We have to care in a special way for children and for grandparents. Children and young people are the future; they are our strength; they are what keep us moving forward. They are the ones in whom we put our hope. Grandparents are a family's memory. They are the ones who gave us the faith, they passed the faith on to us. Taking care of grandparents and taking care of children is the sign of love—I'm not sure if it is the greatest, but for the family I would say that it is the most promising—because it promises the future. A people incapable of caring for children and caring for the elderly is a people without a future, because it lacks the strength and the memory needed to move forward.

The family is beautiful, but it takes hard work; it brings problems. In the family, sometimes there is fighting. The husband argues with the wife; they get upset with each other, or children get upset with their parents. May I offer a bit of advice: never end the day without making peace in the family. In the family the day cannot end in fighting.

May God bless you. May God give you strength. May God inspire you to keep moving forward. Let us care for the family. Let us defend the family, because there our future is at stake. Thank you. God bless you, and please pray for me.

[In his address to the Festival of Families, presented above, the Holy Father chose to ignore his prepared text and to speak extemporaneously instead. Following the address, the Vatican indicated that the prepared remarks should be considered a part of the official record of the Holy Father's pastoral visit to the United States. These prepared remarks follow.]

Dear Brothers and Sisters,
Dear Families,

First of all, I want to thank the families who were willing to share their life stories with us. Thank you for your witness! It is always a gift to listen to families share their life experiences; it touches our hearts. We feel that they speak to us about things that are very personal and unique, which in some way involve all of us. In listening to their experiences, we can feel ourselves drawn in, challenged as married couples and parents, as children, brothers and sisters, and grandparents.

As I was listening, I was thinking how important it is for us to share our home life and to help one another in this marvelous and challenging task of "being a family."

Being with you makes me think of one of the most beautiful mysteries of our Christian faith. God did not want to come into the world other than through a family. God did not want to draw near to humanity other than through a home. God did not want any other name for himself than Emmanuel (cf. Matt 1:23). He is "God with us." This was his desire from the beginning, his purpose, his constant effort: to say to us: "I am God with you, I am God for you." He is the God who from the very beginning of creation said: "It is not good for man to be alone" (Gen 2:18). We can add: it is not good for woman to be alone, it is not good for children, the elderly or the young to be alone. It is not good. That is why a man leaves his father and mother, and clings to his wife, and the two of them become one flesh (cf. Gen 2:24). The two are meant to be a home, a family.

From time immemorial, in the depths of our heart, we have heard those powerful words: it is not good for you to be alone. The family is the great blessing, the great gift of this "God with us," who did not want to abandon us to the solitude of a life without others, without challenges, without a home.

God does not dream by himself, he tries to do everything "with us." His dream constantly comes true in the dreams of many couples who work to make their life that of a family.

That is why the family is the living symbol of the loving plan of which the Father once dreamed. To want to form a family is to resolve to be a part of God's dream, to choose to dream with him, to want to build with him, to join him in this saga of building a world where no one will feel alone, unwanted or homeless.

As Christians, we appreciate the beauty of the family and of family life as the place where we come to learn the meaning and value of human relationships. We learn that "to love someone is not just a strong feeling—it is a decision, it is a judgment, it is a promise" (Erich Fromm, *The Art of Loving*). We learn to stake everything on another person, and we learn that it is worth it.

Jesus was not a confirmed bachelor, far from it! He took the Church as his bride, and made her a people of his own. He laid down his life for those he loved, so that his bride, the Church, could always know that he is God with us, his people, his family. We cannot understand Christ without his Church, just as we cannot understand the Church without her spouse, Christ Jesus, who gave his life out of love, and who makes us see that it is worth the price.

Laying down one's life out of love is not easy. As with the Master, "staking everything" can sometimes involve the cross. Times when everything seems uphill. I think of all those parents, all those families who lack employment or workers' rights, and how this is a true cross. How many sacrifices they make to earn their daily bread! It is understandable that, when these parents return home, they are so weary that they cannot give their best to their children.

I think of all those families which lack housing or live in overcrowded conditions. Families which lack the basics to be able to build bonds of closeness, security and protection from troubles of any kind.

I think of all those families which lack access to basic health services. Families which, when faced with medical problems, especially those of their younger or older members, are dependent on a system which fails to meet their needs, is insensitive to their pain, and forces them to make great sacrifices to receive adequate treatment.

We cannot call any society healthy when it does not leave real room for family life. We cannot think that a society has a future when it fails to pass laws capable of protecting families and ensuring their basic needs, especially those of families just starting out. How many problems would be solved if our societies protected families and provided households, especially those of recently married couples, with the possibility of dignified work, housing and healthcare services to accompany them throughout life.

God's dream does not change; it remains intact and it invites us to work for a society which supports families. A society where bread, "fruit of the earth and the work of human hands" continues to be put on the table of every home, to nourish the hope of its children.

Let us help one another to make it possible to "stake everything on love." Let us help one another at times of difficulty and lighten each other's burdens. Let us support one another. Let us be families which are a support for other families.

Perfect families do not exist. This must not discourage us. Quite the opposite. Love is something we learn; love is something we live; love grows as it is "forged" by the concrete situations which each particular family experiences. Love is born and constantly develops amid lights and shadows. Love can flourish in men and women who try not to make conflict the last word, but rather a new opportunity. An opportunity to seek help, an opportunity to question how we need to improve, an opportunity to discover the God who is with us and never abandons us. This is a great legacy that we can give to our children, a very good lesson: we make mistakes, yes; we have problems, yes. But we know that that is not really what counts. We know that mistakes, problems and conflicts are an opportunity to draw closer to others, to draw closer to God.

This evening we have come together to pray, to pray as a family, to make our homes the joyful face of the Church. To meet that God who did not want to come into our world in any other way than through a family. To meet "God with us," the God who is always in our midst.

— • — 16 — • —

Meeting with Victims of Sexual Abuse
Address of the Holy Father

*St. Charles Borromeo Seminary, Philadelphia
Sunday, September 27, 2015*

My dearest brothers and sisters in Christ, I am grateful for this opportunity to meet you, I am blessed by your presence. Thank you for coming here today.

Words cannot fully express my sorrow for the abuse you suffered. You are precious children of God who should always expect our protection, our care and our love. I am profoundly sorry that your innocence was violated by those who you trusted. In some cases the trust was betrayed by members of your own family, in other cases by priests who carry a sacred responsibility for the care of souls. In all circumstances, the betrayal was a terrible violation of human dignity.

For those who were abused by a member of the clergy, I am deeply sorry for the times when you or your family spoke out, to report the abuse, but you were not heard or believed. Please know that the Holy Father hears you and believes you. I deeply regret that some bishops failed in their responsibility to protect children. It is very disturbing to know that in some cases bishops even were abusers. I pledge to you that we will follow the path of truth wherever it may lead. Clergy and bishops will be held accountable when they abuse or fail to protect children.

We are gathered here in Philadelphia to celebrate God's gift of family life. Within our family of faith and our human families, the sins and crimes of sexual abuse of children must no longer be held in secret and in shame. As we anticipate the Jubilee Year of Mercy, your presence, so generously given despite the anger and pain you have experienced, reveals the merciful heart of Christ. Your stories of survival, each unique and compelling, are powerful signs of the hope that comes from the Lord's promise to be with us always.

It is good to know that you have brought family members and friends with you today. I am grateful for their compassionate support and pray that many people of the Church will respond to the call to accompany those who have suffered abuse. May the Door of Mercy be opened wide in our dioceses, our parishes, our homes and our hearts, to receive those who were abused and to seek the path to forgiveness by trusting in the Lord. We promise to support your continued healing and to always be vigilant to protect the children of today and tomorrow.

When the disciples who walked with Jesus on the road to Emmaus recognized that He was the Risen Lord, they asked Jesus to stay with them. Like those disciples, I humbly beg you and all survivors of abuse to stay with us, to stay with the Church, and that together, as pilgrims on the journey of faith, we might find our way to the Father.

— · — 17 — · —

Meeting with Bishops Taking Part in the World Meeting of Families

Address of the Holy Father

St. Charles Borromeo Seminary,
Chapel of Saint Martin, Philadelphia
Sunday, September 27, 2015

Dear Brother Bishops,

Good morning. I am deeply pained by the stories, the sufferings and the pain of minors who were sexually abused by priests. I continue to be ashamed that persons charged with the tender care of those little ones abused them and caused them grave harm. I deeply regret this. God weeps. The crimes and sins of sexual abuse of minors may no longer be kept secret; I commit myself to ensuring that the Church makes every effort to protect minors and I promise that those responsible will be held to account. Survivors of abuse have become true heralds of hope and ministers of mercy; humbly we owe our gratitude to each of them and to their families for their great courage in shedding the light of Christ on the evil sexual abuse of minors. I say this because I have just met with a group of persons abused as children, who are helped and accompanied here in Philadelphia with particular care by Archbishop Chaput, and we felt that I should communicate this to you.

I am happy to be able to share these moments of pastoral reflection with you, amid the joyful celebrations for the World Meeting of Families. I am speaking in Spanish because they told me that you all know Spanish.

For the Church, the family is not first and foremost a cause for concern, but rather the joyous confirmation of God's blessing upon the masterpiece of creation. Every day, all over the world, the Church can rejoice in the Lord's gift of so many families who, even amid difficult trials, remain faithful to their promises and keep the faith!

I would say that the foremost pastoral challenge of our changing times is to move decisively towards recognizing this gift. For all the obstacles we see before us, gratitude and appreciation should prevail over concerns and complaints. The family is the fundamental locus of the covenant between the Church and God's creation, with that creation which God blessed on the last day with a family. Without the family, not even the Church would exist. Nor could she be what she is called to be, namely "a sign and instrument of communion with God and of the unity of the entire human race" (*Lumen Gentium* 1).

Needless to say, our understanding, shaped by the interplay of ecclesial faith and the conjugal experience of sacramental grace, must not lead us to disregard the unprecedented changes taking place in contemporary society, with their social, cultural—and, sadly, also legal—effects on family bonds. These changes affect all of us, believers and nonbelievers alike. Christians are not "immune" to the changes of their times. This concrete world, with all its many problems and possibilities, is where we must live, believe and proclaim.

Until recently, we lived in a social context where the similarities between the civil institution of marriage and the Christian sacrament were considerable and shared. The two were interrelated and mutually supportive. This is no longer the case. To describe our situation today, I would use two familiar images: our neighborhood stores and our large supermarkets.

There was a time when one neighborhood store had everything one needed for personal and family life. The products may not have been cleverly displayed, or offered much choice, but there was a personal bond between the shopkeeper and his customers. Business was done on the basis of trust, people knew one another, they were all neighbors. They trusted one another. They built up trust. These stores were often simply known as "the local market."

Then a different kind of store grew up: the supermarket. Huge spaces with a great selection of merchandise. The world seems to have become one of these great supermarkets; our culture has become more and more competitive. Business is no longer conducted on the basis of trust; others can no longer be trusted. There are no longer close personal relationships. Today's culture seems to encourage people not to bond with anything or anyone, not to trust. The most important thing nowadays seems to be following the latest trend or activity. This is even true of religion. Today consumption seems to determine what is important. Consuming relationships, consuming friendships, consuming religions, consuming, consuming. . . . Whatever the cost or consequences. A consumption which does not favor bonding, a consumption which has little to do with human relationships. Social bonds are a mere "means" for the satisfaction of "my needs." The important thing is no longer our neighbor, with his or her familiar face, story and personality.

The result is a culture which discards everything that is no longer "useful" or "satisfying" for the tastes of the consumer. We have turned our society into a huge multicultural showcase tied only to the tastes of certain "consumers," while so many others only "eat the crumbs which fall from their masters' table" (Matt 15:27).

This causes great harm; it greatly wounds our culture. I dare say that at the root of so many contemporary situations is a kind of impoverishment born of a widespread and radical sense of loneliness. Running after the latest fad, accumulating "friends" on one of the social networks, we get caught up in what contemporary society has to offer. Loneliness with fear of commitment in a limitless effort to feel recognized.

Should we blame our young people for having grown up in this kind of society? Should we condemn them for living in this kind of a world? Should they hear their pastors saying that "it was all better back then," "the world is falling apart and if things go on this way, who knows where we will end up"? It makes me think of an Argentine tango! No, I do not think that this is the way. As shepherds following in the footsteps of the Good Shepherd, we are asked to seek out, to accompany, to lift up, to bind up the wounds of our time. To look at things realistically, with the eyes of one who feels called to action, to pastoral conversion. The world today demands this pastoral conversion on our part. "It is vitally important for the Church today to go forth and preach the Gospel to all: to all places, on all occasions, without hesitation, reluctance or fear. The joy of the Gospel is for all people: no one can be excluded" (*Evangelii Gaudium* 23). The Gospel is not a product to be consumed; it is not a part of this culture of consumption.

We would be mistaken, however, to see this "culture" of the present world as mere indifference towards marriage and the family, as pure and simple selfishness. Are today's young people hopelessly timid, weak, inconsistent? We must not fall into this trap. Many young people, in the context of this culture of discouragement, have yielded to a form of unconscious acquiescence. They are afraid, deep down, paralyzed before the beautiful, noble and truly necessary challenges. Many put off marriage while waiting for ideal conditions, when everything can be perfect. Meanwhile, life goes on, without really being lived to the full. For knowledge of life's true pleasures only comes as the fruit of a long-term, generous investment of our intelligence, enthusiasm and passion.

Addressing Congress, a few days ago, I said that we are living in a culture which pressures some young people not to start a family because they lack the material means to do so, and others because they are so well off that they are happy as they are. That is the temptation, not to start a family.

As pastors, we bishops are called to collect our energies and to rebuild enthusiasm for making families correspond ever more fully to the blessing of God which they are! We need to invest our energies not so much in rehearsing the problems of the world around us and the merits of Christianity, but in extending a sincere invitation to young people to be brave and to opt for marriage and the family. In Buenos Aires, many women used to complain about their children who were 30, 32 or 34 years old and still single: "I don't know what to do"—"Well, stop ironing their shirts!" Young people have to be encouraged to take this risk, but it is a risk of fruitfulness and life.

Here too, we need a bit of holy *parrhesia* on the part of bishops. "Why aren't you married?" "Yes, I have a fiancée, but we don't know . . . maybe yes, maybe no. . . . We're saving some money for the party, for this or that. . . ." The holy *parrhesia* to accompany them and make them grow towards the commitment of marriage.

A Christianity which "does" little in practice, while incessantly "explaining" its teachings, is dangerously unbalanced. I would even say that it is stuck in a vicious circle. A pastor must show that the "Gospel of the family" is truly "good news" in a world where self-concern seems to reign supreme! We are not speaking about some romantic dream: the perseverance which is called for in having a family and raising it transforms the world and human history. Families transform the world and history.

A pastor serenely yet passionately proclaims the word of God. He encourages believers to aim high. He will enable his brothers and sisters to hear and experience God's promise, which can expand their experience of motherhood and fatherhood within the horizon of a new "familiarity" with God (Mark 3:31-35).

A pastor watches over the dreams, the lives and the growth of his flock. This "watchfulness" is not the result of talking but of shepherding. Only one capable of standing "in the midst of" the flock can be watchful, not someone who is afraid of questions, afraid of contact and accompaniment. A pastor keeps watch first and foremost with prayer, supporting the faith of his people and instilling confidence in the Lord, in his presence. A pastor remains vigilant by helping people to lift their gaze at times of discouragement, frustration and failure. We might well ask whether in our pastoral ministry we are ready to "waste" time with families. Whether we are ready to be present to them, sharing their difficulties and joys.

Naturally, experiencing the spirit of this joyful familiarity with God, and then spreading its powerful evangelical fruitfulness, has to be the primary feature of our lifestyle as bishops: a lifestyle of prayer and preaching the Gospel (Acts 6:4). I have always been struck by how, in the early days of the Church, the Hellenists complained that their widows and orphans were not being well cared for. The apostles, of course, weren't able to handle this themselves, so they got together and came up with deacons. The Holy Spirit inspired them to create deacons and when Peter announced the decision, he explained: "We are going to choose seven men to take care of this; for our part, we have two responsibilities: prayer and preaching." What is the first job of bishops? To pray. The second job goes along with this: to preach. We are helped by this dogmatic definition. Unless I am wrong, Cardinal Müller helps us because he defines what is the role of the bishop. The bishop is charged to be a pastor, but to be a pastor first and foremost by his prayer and preaching, because everything else follows, if there is time.

By our own humble Christian apprenticeship in the familial virtues of God's people, we will become more and more like fathers and mothers (as did Saint Paul: cf. 1 Thess 2:7, 11), and less like people who have simply learned to live without a family. Lack of contact with families makes us people who learn to live without a family, and this is not good. Our ideal is not to live without love! A good pastor renounces the love of a family precisely in order to focus all his energies, and the grace of his particular vocation, on the evangelical blessing of the love of men and women who carry forward God's plan of creation, beginning with those who are lost, abandoned, wounded, broken, downtrodden and deprived of their dignity. This total surrender to God's *agape* is certainly not a vocation lacking in tenderness and affection! We need but look to Jesus to understand this (cf. Matt 19:12). The mission of a good pastor, in the style of God—and only God can authorize this, not our own presumption!—imitates in every way and for all people the Son's love for the Father. This is reflected in the tenderness with which a pastor devotes himself to the loving care of the men and women of our human family.

For the eyes of faith, this is a most valuable sign. Our ministry needs to deepen the covenant between the Church and the family. I repeat this: to deepen the covenant between the Church and the family. Otherwise it becomes arid, and the human family will grow irremediably distant, by our own fault, from God's joyful good news, and will go to the latest supermarket to buy whatever product suits them then and there.

If we prove capable of the demanding task of reflecting God's love, cultivating infinite patience and serenity as we strive to sow its seeds in the frequently crooked furrows in which we are called to plant—for very often we really do have to sow in crooked furrows—then even a Samaritan woman with five "non-husbands" will discover that she is capable of giving witness. And for every rich young man who with sadness feels that he has to calmly keep considering the matter, an older publican will come down from the tree and give fourfold to the poor, to whom, before that moment, he had never even given a thought.

My brothers, may God grant us this gift of a renewed closeness between the family and the Church. Families need it, the Church needs it, and we pastors need it.

The family is our ally, our window to the world; the family is the proof of an irrevocable blessing of God destined for all the children who in every age are born into this difficult yet beautiful creation which God has asked us to serve! Thank you.

18

Visit to Detainees

Address of the Holy Father

Curran-Fromhold Correctional Facility, Philadelphia
Sunday, September 27, 2015

Dear Brothers and Sisters,

Good morning. I am going to speak in Spanish because I don't speak English, but he [pointing to the interpreter] speaks good English and he is going to translate for me. Thank you for receiving me and giving me the opportunity to be here with you and to share this time in your lives. It is a difficult time, one full of struggles. I know it is a painful time not only for you, but also for your families and for all of society. Any society, any family, which cannot share or take seriously the pain of its children, and views that pain as something normal or to be expected, is a society "condemned" to remain a hostage to itself, prey to the very things which cause that pain.

I am here as a pastor, but above all as a brother, to share your situation and to make it my own. I have come so that we can pray together and offer our God everything that causes us pain, but also everything that gives us hope, so that we can receive from him the power of the resurrection.

I think of the Gospel scene where Jesus washes the feet of his disciples at the Last Supper. This was something his disciples found hard to accept. Even Peter refused, and told him: "You will never wash my feet" (John 13:8).

In those days, it was the custom to wash someone's feet when they came to your home. That was how they welcomed people. The roads were not paved, they were covered with dust, and little stones would get stuck in your sandals. Everyone walked those roads, which left their feet dusty, bruised or cut from those stones. That is why we see Jesus washing feet, our feet, the feet of his disciples, then and now.

We all know that life is a journey, along different roads, different paths, which leave their mark on us.

We also know in faith that Jesus seeks us out. He wants to heal our wounds, to soothe our feet which hurt from travelling alone, to wash each of us clean of the dust from our journey. He doesn't ask us where we have been, he doesn't question us what about we have done. Rather, he tells us: "Unless I wash your feet, you have no share with me" (John 13:8). Unless I wash your feet, I will not be able to give you the life which the Father always dreamed of, the life for which he created you. Jesus comes to meet us, so that he can restore our dignity as children of God. He wants to help us to set out again, to resume our journey, to recover our hope, to restore our faith and trust. He wants us to keep walking along the paths of life, to realize that we have a mission, and that confinement is never the same thing as exclusion.

Life means "getting our feet dirty" from the dust-filled roads of life and history. All of us need to be cleansed, to be washed. All of us. Myself, first and foremost. All of us are being sought out by the Teacher, who wants to help us resume our journey. The Lord goes in search of us; to all of us he stretches out a helping hand.

It is painful when we see prison systems which are not concerned to care for wounds, to soothe pain, to offer new possibilities. It is painful when we see people who think that only others need to be cleansed, purified, and do not recognize that their weariness, pain and wounds are also the weariness, pain and wounds of society. The Lord tells us this clearly with a sign: he washes our feet so we can come back to the table. The table from which he wishes no one to be excluded. The table which is spread for all and to which all of us are invited.

This time in your life can only have one purpose: to give you a hand in getting back on the right road, to give you a hand to help you rejoin society. All of us are part of that effort, all of us are invited to encourage, help and enable your rehabilitation. A rehabilitation which everyone seeks and desires: inmates and their families, correctional authorities, social and educational programs. A rehabilitation which benefits and elevates the morale of the entire community and society.

I encourage you to have this attitude with one another and with all those who in any way are part of this institution. May you make possible new opportunities; may you blaze new trails, new paths.

All of us have something we need to be cleansed of, or purified from. All of us. May the knowledge of this fact inspire us all to live in solidarity, to support one another and seek the best for others.

Let us look to Jesus, who washes our feet. He is "the way, and the truth, and the life." He comes to save us from the lie that says no one can change, the lie of thinking that no one can change. Jesus helps us to journey along the paths of life and fulfillment. May the power of his love and his resurrection always be a path leading you to new life.

Just as we are, seated, let us silently ask the Lord to bless us. May the Lord bless you and keep you. May he make his face shine upon you and be gracious to you. May he lift up his countenance upon you and give you peace. Thank you.

Impromptu comments at the end of the meeting:
The chair you made is very nice, very beautiful. Thanks for your work.

$$\cdot - = 19 = - \cdot$$

Closing Mass
of the Eighth World Meeting of Families
Homily of His Holiness Pope Francis

Benjamin Franklin Parkway, Philadelphia
Sunday, September 27, 2015

Today the word of God surprises us with powerful and thought-provoking images. Images which challenge us, but also stir our enthusiasm.

In the first reading, Joshua tells Moses that two members of the people are prophesying, speaking God's word, without a mandate. In the Gospel, John tells Jesus that the disciples had stopped someone from casting out evil spirits in the name of Jesus. Here is the surprise: Moses and Jesus both rebuke those closest to them for being so narrow! Would that all could be prophets of God's word! Would that everyone could work miracles in the Lord's name!

Jesus encountered hostility from people who did not accept what he said and did. For them, his openness to the honest and sincere faith of many men and women who were not part of God's chosen people seemed intolerable. The disciples, for their part, acted in good faith. But the temptation to be scandalized by the freedom of God, who sends rain on the righteous and the unrighteous alike (Matt 5:45), bypassing bureaucracy, official-

96

dom and inner circles, threatens the authenticity of faith. Hence it must be vigorously rejected.

Once we realize this, we can understand why Jesus' words about causing "scandal" are so harsh. For Jesus, the truly "intolerable" scandal is everything that breaks down and destroys our trust in the working of the Spirit!

Our Father will not be outdone in generosity and he continues to scatter seeds. He scatters the seeds of his presence in our world, for "love consists in this, not that we have loved God but that *he loved us*" first (1 John 4:10). That love gives us the profound certainty that we are sought by God; he waits for us. It is this confidence which makes disciples encourage, support and nurture the good things happening all around them. God wants all his children to take part in the feast of the Gospel. Jesus says, "Do not hold back anything that is good, instead help it to grow!" To raise doubts about the working of the Spirit, to give the impression that it cannot take place in those who are not "part of our group," who are not "like us," is a dangerous temptation. Not only does it block conversion to the faith; it is a perversion of faith!

Faith opens a "window" to the presence and working of the Spirit. It shows us that, like happiness, holiness is always tied to little gestures. "Whoever gives you a cup of water in my name will not go unrewarded," says Jesus (cf. Mark 9:41). These little gestures are those we learn at home, in the family; they get lost amid all the other things we do, yet they do make each day different. They are the quiet things done by mothers and grandmothers, by fathers and grandfathers, by children, by brothers and sisters. They are little signs of tenderness, affection and compassion. Like the warm supper we look forward to at night, the early lunch awaiting someone who gets up early to go to work. Homely gestures. Like a blessing before we go to bed, or a hug after we return from a hard day's work. Love is shown by little things, by attention to small daily signs which make us feel at home. Faith grows when it is lived and shaped by love. That is why our families, our homes, are true domestic churches. They are the right place for faith to become life, and life to grow in faith.

Jesus tells us not to hold back these little miracles. Instead, he wants us to encourage them, to spread them. He asks us to go through life, our everyday life, encouraging all these little signs of love as signs of his own living and active presence in our world.

So we might ask ourselves, today, here, at the conclusion of this meeting: How are we trying to live this way in our homes, in our societies? What kind of world do we want to leave to our children (cf. *Laudato Sì* 160)? We cannot answer these questions alone, by ourselves. It is the Spirit who challenges us to respond as part of the great human family. Our common house can no longer tolerate sterile divisions. The urgent challenge of protecting our home includes the effort to bring the entire human family together in the pursuit of a sustainable and integral development, for we know that things can change (cf. ibid., 13). May our children find in us models and incentives to communion, not division! May our children find in us men and women capable of joining others in bringing to full flower all the good seeds which the Father has sown!

Pointedly, yet affectionately, Jesus tells us: "If you, who are evil, know how to give good gifts to your children, how much more will the heavenly Father give the Holy Spirit to those who ask him!" (Luke 11:13). How much wisdom there is in these few words! It is true that, as far as goodness and purity of heart are concerned, we human beings don't have much to show! But Jesus knows that, where children are concerned, we are capable of boundless generosity. So he reassures us: if only we have faith, the Father will give us his Spirit.

We Christians, the Lord's disciples, ask the families of the world to help us! How many of us are here at this celebration! This is itself something prophetic, a kind of miracle in today's world, which is tired of inventing new divisions, new hurts, new disasters. Would that we could all be prophets! Would that all of us could be open to miracles of love to benefit our own families and all the families of the world, and thus overcome the scandal of a narrow, petty love, closed in on itself, impatient of others! I leave you with a question for each of you to answer—because I said the word "impatient": at home do we shout at one another or do we speak with love and tenderness? This is a good way of measuring our love.

And how beautiful it would be if everywhere, even beyond our borders, we could appreciate and encourage this prophecy and this miracle! We renew our faith in the word of the Lord which invites faithful families to this openness. It invites all those who want to share the prophecy of the covenant of man and woman, which generates life and reveals God! May the Lord help us to be sharers in the prophecy of peace, of tenderness and affection in the family. May his word help us to share in the prophetic sign of watching over our children and our grandparents with tenderness, with patience and with love.

Anyone who wants to bring into this world a family which teaches children to be excited by every gesture aimed at overcoming evil—a family which shows that the Spirit is alive and at work—will encounter our gratitude and our appreciation. Whatever the family, people, religion or region to which they belong!

May God grant that all of us may be prophets of the joy of the Gospel, the Gospel of the family and family love, as disciples of the Lord. May he grant us the grace to be worthy of that purity of heart which is not scandalized by the Gospel! Amen.

POSTSCRIPT

SEPTEMBER 27, 2015

—·—20—·—

In-Flight Press Conference
of His Holiness Pope Francis
from the United States
of America to Rome

Papal Flight
Sunday, September 27, 2015

Father Lombardi:
Your Holiness, we welcome you here. Thank you for once again taking time now after such a demanding and tiring journey. So we will get right to our questions. The first person is this young lady here, who wrote a piece about you for *Time* magazine, so she is well informed about your visit to America. She will ask her question in English, and Matteo will translate it into Italian.

Pope Francis:
Good evening everyone, and thank you so much for your work, because you were all over the place! I was in the car, but you. . . . So thank you very much.

Elizabeth Dias, correspondent for *Time Magazine*:
Thank you, Holy Father: I am Elizabeth Dias, correspondent for *Time* magazine. We are curious to know . . . this was your first

visit to the United States. What surprised you about the United States, and what differed from your expectations?

Pope Francis:
Well, it was my first visit: I had never been here before. I was surprised by the warmth of the people, who were so kind: something beautiful but also different. In Washington the welcome was warm but a little more formal; in New York it was rather exuberant; in Philadelphia, it was very heartfelt. Three different expressions, but the same welcome! I was very struck by people's kindness, by their welcome; and also in the religious ceremonies by their devotion, their sense of faith. . . . People could be seen praying, and this made a great impression on me. It's beautiful.

Elizabeth Dias:
Was there any unexpected challenge from the United States? Any provocation?

Pope Francis:
No, thank God, no, no. . . . Everything went well. No challenges. No provocations. Everyone was very polite. Nothing offensive, no negative things. But as for challenges, we keep working with these faithful people, as in the past, helping them to grow, being there for them in good times and in bad, amid hardships, when there is no work, amid sickness. . . . The challenge for the Church today is what it always has been: to be close to people, close to people in the United States, not to be a Church cut off from people . . . but close. And this is a challenge which the Church in the United States recognizes and is working at.

Father Lombardi:
The second question is from David O'Reilly of the *Philadelphia Inquirer*, one of the major papers in Philadelphia, where we have been in these days.

David O'Reilly, *Philadelphia Inquirer*:
Holy Father, Philadelphia—as you know—has passed through a painful period with sexual abuse; it's still an open wound in Philadelphia. I know that many people in Philadelphia were surprised that you in your address to the bishops, in Washington, you offered them encouragement and support. I think that many people in Philadelphia would like to ask you: "Why did you feel the need to offer the bishops encouragement and support?"

Pope Francis:
In Washington I spoke to all the bishops of the United States; they were all there, from the whole country. I felt the need to express empathy, because something really terrible took place, and many of them suffered because they weren't aware of it, or when it came out, they suffered, as men of the Church, men of prayer, true pastors. . . . And I said that I knew that they—I used a word from the Bible, from the Book of Revelation: "You are coming from the great tribulation." What happened was a great tribulation. But not only emotional suffering. This is what I said today to those who suffered abuse. It was . . . I won't say *apostasy*, but almost a *sacrilege*. We know that abuse is everywhere: in families, in neighborhoods, in schools, in gyms, everywhere. But when a priest commits abuse, it is extremely grave, because the vocation of the priest is to help that boy or girl to aim high, to grow in the love of God, to grow to affective maturity and goodness. And instead of that, he crushed them, which is evil. That is why it is practically a sacrilege. He betrayed his vocation, the Lord's call. That is why the Church is now working hard on this. These things must not be covered up; and those who covered them up are also guilty, even some bishops who covered them up. It is a terrible thing. My words of support were not intended to say: "Don't worry about it; it's nothing!" They were more like: "This was so terrible that I imagine that you wept greatly over it." That was the sense of my words. And I had strong words today.

Father Lombardi:
Thank you very much. Now I ask Maria Antonietta Collins and Andrés Beltramo Alvarez to approach for the next questions.

Maria Antonietta Collins:
Holy Father, you have spoken a great deal about forgiveness, how God forgives us and how we are the ones who often have to ask forgiveness. I would like to ask you, after having seen you today at the seminary: there are many priests who sexually abused minors and have not asked forgiveness from their victims. Do you forgive them? And do you understand, on the other hand, the victims and their relatives who cannot, or do not want, to forgive?

Pope Francis:
If a person has done wrong, and is conscious of what he has done, but does not beg forgiveness, I ask God to take this into account. I forgive him, but he does not accept forgiveness, he is closed to forgiveness. It is one thing to forgive—we are bound to forgive, because we have all been forgiven—but it is another thing to accept forgiveness. If that priest is closed to forgiveness, he will not receive it, because he has locked the door from the inside; all that remains is to pray that the Lord will open that door. We must be ready to forgive, but not all can receive it or are able or willing to receive it. What I'm saying is harsh. But this explains why some people finish their lives badly, without receiving God's tender mercy. And your second question?

Maria Antonietta Collins:
Whether you understand victims and relatives who find themselves unable to forgive, or who do not want to forgive?

Pope Francis:
Yes, I understand them. I understand them, I pray for them and I do not judge them. Once, in one of these meetings, I met several people, and one woman said to me: "When my mother found out that I had been abused, she blasphemed God; she lost her faith

and died an atheist." I understand that woman. I understand her, and God, who is better than I am, understands her. I am certain that God has welcomed that woman, because what was touched, what was destroyed, was her own flesh, the flesh of her daughter. I understand that. I do not judge someone who cannot forgive. I pray and I ask God, because God is a master at finding a way to resolve things. I ask him to take care of it.

Father Lombardi:
Andrés Beltramo, of *Notimex*, who will perhaps ask his question in Italian; that way it helps all of us.

Andrés Beltramo:
Father, thank you, first of all, for this moment. We have all heard you speak so much about the peace process in Colombia, between FARC and the government. Now there is an historic agreement. Do you feel somehow a part of this agreement? You have also said that you were thinking of going to Colombia when this agreement would come about: there are many Colombians who now expect you. . . . One other little question: How do you feel after such an intense trip, once the airplane takes off? Thank you, Father.

Pope Francis:
First, when I heard the news that the agreement would be signed in March, I said to the Lord: "Lord, help us reach March; help us get there with this beautiful wish, because some small things still have to be done, but the will is there. On both sides. It is there. Even on the part of the small group, all three are in agreement. We have to reach March for the definitive accord. That was the point of international justice, as you know. I was very pleased. And I feel like I was part of it in the sense that I have always desired this, and I spoke twice with President Santos about the problem. And the Holy See . . . not just myself, but the Holy See is very willing to help as much as possible.

The other thing. This is a bit personal, but I have to be honest. When the plane leaves after a visit, I think of the faces of all those people. I get the urge to pray for them and to say to the Lord: "I came here to do some good; perhaps I have done wrong, forgive me. But watch over all those people who saw me, who thought about the things I said, who heard me, even those who criticized me, all of them. . . ." This is what I feel. I don't know. That's what I feel. But it's a bit—sorry—personal: you can't say this in the newspapers. . . .

Father Lombardi:
Thank you very much. Thomas Jansen of CIC, the German Catholic Agency.

Thomas Jansen:
Holy Father, I wanted to ask about the immigrant crisis in Europe. Many countries are building new fences out of barbed wire. What do you think about this development?

Pope Francis:
You used a word: "crisis." A state of crisis comes about as the result of a long process. This is a process which has been brewing for years, because the wars which those people are fleeing have been going on for years. Hunger. Hunger has been going on for years. When I think of Africa—this is a bit simplistic, but I give it as an example—I get to thinking: Africa, the exploited continent. They went after slaves there, and then so many resources. The exploited continent. And now, wars, tribal and not, have economic interests behind them. And I think that, rather than exploiting a continent or a nation or a land, invest there, so that those people can have work and the crisis can be avoided. It is true: this is a refugee crisis—as I said in the Congress—unprecedented since the aftermath of World War II, the largest of them. You ask me about fences, walls. You know what happens to walls, all of them. Walls all fall down—today, tomorrow or in a hundred years—but they will fall. Building walls is not a solution; a wall is not a solution. Europe is presently in difficulty, this is true. We have to think; we have to understand why this great wave of migration is taking place, and it is not easy to come up with solutions. But dialogue

among countries, that is how solutions can be found. Walls are
never solutions, but bridges always are. I don't know. What do
I think about walls and the barriers . . . whether they last for a
short or a long time . . . they are not a solution. The problem
remains, and hatred grows. That's what I think.

Father Lombardi:
Jean-Marie Guénois of *Figaro*, from the French group.

Jean-Marie Guénois:
Holy Father, obviously you cannot anticipate the debates of the
Synod Fathers; we realize that, but we want to know before the
Synod if in your heart as a pastor, you really want a solution
for the divorced and remarried. We also want to know if your
Motu Proprio on the easing of the annulment process has, to
your mind, closed this debate. Finally, how do you respond to
those who fear that this reform has de facto created "Catholic
divorce"? Thank you.

Pope Francis:
I'll start with the last question. In the reform of the procedures
and means, I closed the door to the administrative process, which
was the way that divorce could have crept in. You could say that
those who are thinking of "Catholic divorce" are mistaken because
this latest document closed the door to divorce. It would have
been easier with the administrative process. There will always be
the judicial process. Then, to continue with your third question:
the document . . . I don't remember if it was the third but you
can correct me. . . .

Jean-Marie Guénois:
The question was on the idea of "Catholic divorce," whether the
Motu Proprio has closed debate on the matter in the Synod?

Pope Francis:
This was something called for by the majority of the Fathers in the
Synod last year: a streamlining of the process since some cases

could last 10 or 15 years. There is one sentence, then another, there is one appeal, followed by another. It never ends. The double sentence, in cases where the first sentence was valid and not appealed, was introduced by Pope Benedict XIV Lambertini, because in central Europe (I won't say which country), there were abuses and to stop this he had introduced this, but it is not essential to the process. Procedures change, jurisprudence changes, it constantly improves. At the time there was a need to do this. Later, Pius X wanted to streamline (the process); he started, but he didn't have the time or opportunity to continue. The Synod Fathers asked that the procedures of marriage nullity be streamlined. I will leave it at that. The Motu Proprio speeds up the procedures, but it is not divorce, because a sacramental marriage is indissoluble. This is not something the Church can change. It is doctrine; as a sacrament, marriage is indissoluble. The legal process for establishing that what seemed to be a sacrament was not, because of lack of freedom, for example, or lack of maturity, or mental illness. . . . There are any number of reasons that, after careful investigation, lead to the conclusion that there was no sacrament in a given case. For example, because the person was not free. Another example: now it's less common, but in some sectors of society it was common, at least in Buenos Aires, that when the fiancée got pregnant, they were told they had to get married. In Buenos Aires, I strongly urged, I practically forbade, my priests to celebrate such "shotgun" marriages. They take place to keep up appearances. Then the babies are born and some marriages work out, but there's no freedom. And then things go wrong, they separate. "I was forced to get married because I had to cover up the situation." This is a cause for nullity. There are many others; you can find (a list of) them on the Internet; they are all there.

Then there is the issue of second marriages, the divorced who enter a new union. Read what is in the "Instrumentum Laboris," what is up for discussion. It seems to me somewhat simplistic to state that the Synod . . . that the solution for these people is for them to receive communion. That is not the only solution. . . . No. What the "Instrumentum Laboris" proposes is much more. The problem of new unions on the part of the divorced is not the only problem. The "Instrumentum Laboris" mentions many others. For example, young people are not getting married. They don't want to get married. This is a pastoral problem for the Church. Another problem: the affective maturity needed for marriage. Still another problem is faith: "Do I really believe that this is forever?" "Yes, yes, I believe," but do you really believe it? The preparation for a wedding. I often think that the preparation for becoming a priest takes eight years, and then, it is not definitive; the Church can remove the clerical state. But for marriage, which is for life, we offer four courses, four meetings. . . . Something is not right. The Synod will have to consider carefully how to prepare couples for marriage. This is one of the hardest things. There are many problems; these are all listed in the "Instrumentum Laboris." I am glad you asked about "Catholic divorce." No, it doesn't exist. Either there was no marriage—and this is nullity, that it did not exist—or, if there was a marriage, it is indissoluble. This is clear. Thank you.

Father Lombardi:
Thank you, Holy Father. Now it is the turn of Terry Moran of ABC News, one of the great American networks.

Terry Morgan:
Holy Father, thank you very much, and thanks to the Vatican staff as well. Holy Father, you visited the Little Sisters of the Poor, and we were told that you wanted to show your support for the Sisters, also in their court case. Holy Father, do you also support those individuals, including government officials, who say they cannot in good conscience, their personal conscience, comply with certain laws or carry out their duties as government officials, for example in issuing marriage licenses to same-sex couples? Would you support those of claims of religious freedom?

Pope Francis:
I can't foresee every possible case of conscientious objection. But yes, I can say conscientious objection is a right, and enters into

every human right. It is a right, and if a person does not allow for conscientious objection, he or she is denying a right. Every legal system should provide for conscientious objection because it is a right, a human right. Otherwise, we would end up selecting between rights: "this right is good, this one less so." It is a human right. I am always moved when I read, and I have read it many times, when I read the "Chanson de Roland," when there were all these Moors lined up before the baptismal font, and they had to choose between baptism and the sword. They had to choose. They weren't permitted conscientious objection. It's a right and if we want to have peace, we have to respect all rights.

Terry Morgan:
Would that include government officials as well?

Pope Francis:
It is a human right. And if a government official is a human person, he enjoys that right. It is a human right.

Father Lombardi:
Thank you. Now it is the turn of Stefano Maria Paci, of the Italian group Sky News.

Stefano Maria Paci:
Your Holiness, at the UN you used very strong words to denounce the world's silence before the persecution of Christians, who are deprived of their homes and goods, driven out, enslaved and brutally murdered. Yesterday, President Hollande announced that France has started bombing ISIS bases in Syria. What do you think of this military action? Also, out of curiosity: Mayor Marino, the mayor of Rome, the city of the Jubilee, stated that he came to the World Meeting of Families because you invited him. Can you tell us how it went? [Note: The Roman authorities have clarified that Mayor Marino never claimed to have been invited by the Holy Father].

Pope Francis:

I will start with your second question. I did not invite Mayor Marino. Is that clear? I did not invite him, and I asked the organizers and they didn't invite him either. He came. He says he is a Catholic and he came of his own accord. That's what happened. The first thing.

The other question was about bombings. Actually I heard the news the day before yesterday and I haven't read anything about it. I don't know much about the situation. I heard that Russia has taken one position, and that of the United States was not yet clear. I don't know what to say because I haven't fully understood the situation. But when I hear the word "bombing," death, bloodshed. . . . I repeat what I said to Congress and at the UN: these things are to be avoided. But I don't know, I can't judge the political situation because I am not familiar with it. Thank you.

Father Lombardi:

Thank you. Now Miriam Schmidt of Deutsche Presseagentur.

Miriam Schmidt:

Holy Father, I wanted to ask a question about the relationship of the Holy See with China and the situation in that country, which is quite difficult also for the Catholic Church. What are your thoughts?

Pope Francis:

China is a great nation which offers the world a great culture and so many good things. I once said as we were flying over China, returning from Korea, that I would very much like to go to China. I love the Chinese people, I wish them well, and I hope for a possibility of good relations. We do have contacts, we talk, we are moving forward, but for me, having as a friend a country like China, which has a great culture and such opportunity to do good, would be a joy.

Father Lombardi:
Thank you. And now we have Sagrario Ruiz de Apodaca.

Sagrario Ruiz de Apodaca:
Thank you. Good evening, Holy Father. You visited the United States for the first time, never having been there before, you spoke to Congress and the United Nations, and you drew great crowds. Do you feel more powerful? I would also like to ask you, because we heard you speak about the role of religious women and women in the Church in the United States: will we ever see women priests in the Catholic Church, as some groups in the United States are demanding and as is the case in some other Christian Churches?

Pope Francis:
The Sisters in the United States have done wonders in the areas of education and health care. People in the United States love the Sisters. I don't know how much they may love the priests, but they do love the Sisters. They are good women, very good women. Each follows her own Congregation and its rules, there are differences, but they are good and for this reason I felt bound to thank them for what they have done. An important person in the United States government told me in these days: "Whatever education I received, I owe above all to the Sisters." The Sisters have schools in all neighborhoods, rich and poor. They work with the poor in hospitals. . . . This was the first question. I remember the third one, but the second?

Sagrario Ruiz de Apodaca:
Whether you feel powerful after being in the United States, with this agenda and being so successful. . . .

Pope Francis:
I don't know if I was successful or not. But I'm afraid of myself. Because if I am afraid of myself, I always feel, I don't know, weak

in the sense of powerless. Power is also fleeting, here today, gone tomorrow. . . . It's important if you can do good with power. Jesus defined power: true power is service, serving others, serving the poor. And I still have to advance on this path of service, because I feel that I don't do everything I must do. That is how I feel about power.

Third, on women priests, this cannot be done. Pope Saint John Paul II, when the question was being raised, after very lengthy reflection, stated this clearly. Not because women aren't capable, but . . . look, in the Church, women are more important than men, because the Church is a woman. We speak of the Church as "she"; she is the Bride of Christ, and Our Lady is more important than Popes, bishops and priests. I must acknowledge that we are somewhat behind in developing of theology of women. We have to progress in that area. That is certainly true. Thank you.

Father Lombardi:
Now the last question is from Matilde Imberty, of Radio France, and then we finish.

Matilde Imberty:
Holy Father, in the United States you became a celebrity. Is that good for the Church, that the Pope is a celebrity?

Pope Francis:
Do you know what title the Popes used to use, and should still use? "Servant of the servants of God." That is a little different than being a celebrity, a "star." Stars are beautiful to gaze at. I like to gaze at them in the summer, when the sky is clear. But the Pope must be, has to be, the servant of the servants of God. In the media this sort of thing happens. But there is another side to the story. How many stars have we seen shine, then go out and fall. It is something fleeting. Whereas being the servant of servants of God, that is something beautiful. It doesn't pass away. That is what I think.

Father Lombardi:
Good. We have come to the end of the list . . . many thanks for
your availability. We have had about fifty minutes of conversation,
which has been a fair amount of time. Congratulations on the
endurance you have shown throughout this journey and in this
conversation with us. We will continue to follow you. It doesn't
end with this journey. This visit has concluded, but we have the
Synod and so many other things. . . . And we want to keep
following you with great affection, esteem, and appreciation, in
the hope of assisting you in your service of the servants of God.

Pope Francis:
Thank you for your work, for your patience, your kindness. Thank
you. I am at your service. I pray for you, I do. Thanks for your
help. Have a good flight!